THE APOSTLE PETER: HIS WORDS SHOULD BE "RED" TOO!

JAMES A. HOUCK, JR., PH.D.

Copyright © 2009 by James A. Houck, Jr., Ph.D.
houckj@neumann.edu
Department of Pastoral and Theological Studies
Neumann College, Aston, PA 19014-1298

THE APOSTLE PETER:
HIS WORDS SHOULD BE "RED" TOO!
by James A. Houck, Jr., Ph.D.

Printed in the United States of America

ISBN 978-1-60791-569-0

www.xulonpress.com

Dedication

I am truly grateful for my wife, family, friends and collegues for their love and support. And for all who have taught me more about the transforming work of God through their prayers, not by what they say, but through the inaudible spirit of their humility.

"The Apostle Peter:
His Words Should Be Red Too!"

Table of Contents

PREFACE

About the Cover

In the Summer of 1888, Vincent Van Gogh visited Arles in the south of France. It was there that he painted the famous *Fishing Boats on the Beach*. Throughout his life, Van Gogh was often plagued with severe bouts of depression, anxiety, and epilepsy, as well as feelings of worthlessness and despair. His "madness," was often seen in his choice of colors in his paintings, which was his primary form of expression. Van Gogh described the reason for painting these boats. . .

"Spent a week in Saintes-Maries. . .on the really flat sandy beach with small green, red and blue boats, which in their form and colour are as pretty as flowers. One man alone uses them. These skiffs rarely ever go on the high seas. They set off when there is no wind blowing and return to land as soon as the wind becomes too strong."

Van Gogh's description of the boats of Saintes-Maries may also describe our human nature and the call of God.

How many people are eager to follow God initially? Life is exciting, and our faith is strong as we leave what is familiar for unknown lands. Unfortunately, at the first sign of a storm and fierce winds, we turn around and head back for shore, only to blame God for our own misperceptions about what the Christian life should be for us. However, if we are able to stay the course and ride through the storms of life, we discover that not only was God with us all along, but also our struggles have produced perseverance, character and, thus, hope. (Romans 5:3-4).

This analogy also finds a parallel in the field of psychology. A well-known story is told of one of C.G. Jung's clients. She described for him a dream she had one night where she was waist deep in molten lava. The more she struggled to free herself; the more she began to sink. In despair she cried out, "Help me out, Dr. Jung!" By that point, only one shoulder was seen sticking out. Dr. Jung put his hand on her shoulder, pushed her in deeper and said, "Not out, but through." Jung interpreted this dream as his client doing some excellent inner work and encouraged her to continue facing her issues, instead of wanting to be rescued from the pain.

At difficult points in counseling, many people turn back, stating that some memories, dreams and tragic events are just too painful to work through. Yet, having the courage to face a difficult and often traumatic past that has been laden with negative emotions and maladaptive behaviors, not only are people able to get at the heart of such experiences, but also to discover the Holy Spirit's work of transformation. This is not a one-time endeavor; self-examination and transformation is on-going for the rest of our lives.

In essence, this is the goal of Pastoral Counseling. It is about the personal and professional integration of clinical psychology, along with religious, spiritual and theological issues, resulting in a life-giving transformation for both counselor and client. Van Gogh's painting of *Fishing Boats on the Beach* displays a powerful image for many who may find themselves too filled with fear to venture out in deep water.

Hopefully in reading this book you will discover the courage within to examine your life, as well as the humility to help others who may find themselves adrift in the sea of life.

INTRODUCTION

Remember that old riddle? *What's black and white and red all over?* Depending on your age and culture, you could answer either a skunk with a severe case of diaper rash, or a newspaper. But how about this answer: The gospels. That's right. If you have ever thumbed through the gospels, you see certain words and paragraphs that are colored red in some editions. This color indicates that these are the words spoken by Jesus. These words are red because, nestled in the gospel narratives, they are meant to jump out at us and grab our attention. They say to us, "Take notice, because Jesus is speaking!"

Of course, we all know that it's not the color that makes Jesus' words significant. After all, his words could have been printed in blue, green or purple ink. Rather, we give credence to Jesus' words because of what, when, how, and where he said what he did. Jesus' words were not just part of nice stories; his words impacted people where they lived and spoke directly to their brokenness, shame, pride, guilt, confusion, remorse, and joy. Every word is significant because on some level, a spiritual healing and transformation occurred in everyone who heard Jesus' voice and embraced his teaching. Moreover, those listeners were never the same again.

Take the Apostle Peter for example. I don't believe we have a more radical example of spiritual transformation, apart from the Apostle Paul, than with Peter. One of the first things Jesus did when he met Peter in John 1:35-42 was to change his name from Simon to Peter, which means "rock." Interestingly, Peter was anything but a rock in the gospels. Instead, he was extremely unstable, vulnerable and impulsive. Jesus renamed Peter for the potential he saw within him, not for what he was, but rather for what he would become by God's grace. When we read the gospel stories we quickly realize that the Peter portrayed in the gospels is not the same Peter in the Book of Acts. The difference was that on the Day of Pentecost (Acts 2), as the sound of rushing wind and tongues of fire fell on the disciples, a powerful transformation occurred in them. I imagine this transformation was unlike anything the tiny world of Palestine had never seen or heard before. In that moment it was Peter who boldly proclaimed the significance of that moment in light of Christ's death, resurrection and exaltation.

For us today, we can see many similarities between our lives and Peter of the gospels. In many ways his story mirrors ours. For instance, how many times are we unsure of ourselves? How often are we prone to shame and guilt? How often do we become overly enthusiastic, often speak before we think, are rash in our behavior, at times becoming more stubborn than a mule, and may even get a little hot-tempered? More than we would like to admit, I imagine. Yet before we write ourselves off as hopeless, consider this. Jesus never saw Peter as hopeless. What he did see was potential, potential that would be realized through one simple touch of the Holy Spirit. Jesus knew that the rushing winds of Pentecost would make all of the difference in the life of Peter, us, and the world.

For this reason, I believe Peter's words should be red, too, not the deep red that carries the same weight as Jesus' words, but rather a "blush" color that results from getting caught sticking your foot in your mouth time and time again. No doubt we have probably seen that same color on our faces when we are embarrassed, shamed, feel guilty or are aroused with passion. Despite these uncomfortable feelings, this reaction is normal. Think back to your days in health class. Remember that when a person is faced with danger or excitement, immediately the body's autonomic nervous system, or the "fight or flight" response, is triggered, causing the person to experience an increase in our heart rate, sweating, feeling flushed, dry mouth, etc. We often associate these physiological reactions with over-exertion at work, play or when we run a fever. As the body becomes too hot, the brain sends a message for it to return the temperature to normal. To achieve this, the blood vessels in the body begin to widen, bringing blood to the surface of the skin to be cooled down, most notably on the face and neck. Perhaps you've also noticed this reaction when you have eaten hot and spicy foods! However, "blushing" is not just limited to physical activity; it also occurs whenever emotions take over, such as when an individual becomes overly anxious, fearful or self-conscious in social situations.

In mainstream Christianity we often hear a distorted message that our emotions are the enemy, that we should do everything in our power and prayers to eliminate those so-called "dark" emotions, e.g., shame, pride, guilt, anger. In doing so, we will be drawn closer to God as we put to death all the deeds of the flesh. Over the years, mental-health research has shown that a more beneficial way to deal with such emotions is not to deny or dismiss them, but to acknowledge them. Embracing the shadow side and assimilating those dark feelings, so we can work through them, provides a catalyst for emotional and spiritual transformation. If we can sit with those emotions without judging them, they have something to teach us about ourselves, our relationships with others and God. More often than we would like to admit, we want to control God, or at least we want God to be for us who we want God to be, and not who God is. We want God to do things on our timetables, schedules, and according to our plans. After all, it's our lives, right? Not when it comes to following Christ. We are never in a position to dictate to God what we think should occur.

If we are honest with ourselves, we want God to do all the work. How many times have we said: "*If only God would give me patience then I would be able to handle those difficult people.*" What we don't realize is that when we ask for patience, God will bring about those situations which have the potential to develop patience in us. Remember, spiritual fruit takes time to mature.

One of the biggest lessons we must learn is God's order of things. For example, we want the blessings of God, the fruit of the Holy Spirit, transformation and character development, etc. However, what often we don't understand is that these things are a result of consistently embracing life situations which stretch not only our faith, but also the limites of our current understanding of God. In other words, in order to see God more clearly in our lives, God must first remove everything that clouds our vision of Him. In order to hear God more distinctly in our hearts, God must first remove those things, which distract us. In order to love God more intimately, God must first remove those things in our lives that would woo us away from Him (Myss, 2002).

Therefore, the purpose of this book not only is to explore a before and after transformation of Peter by examining his words in the gospels, but also for us to seek transformation by contemplating how his life reflects our own. The exercises at the end of each chapter are intended to help us begin reflecting on and embracing our emotions, through the ancient monastic technique called *lectio divina*, or a contemplate approach to Scripture.

Once regarded as a practice intended solely for those in the monastic community, *lectio divina*, has in the past decade become an increasingly popular way for everyday people to listen to God in prayerful meditation and silence. This discipline may involve changing the way we read Scripture. For example, most of us are comfortable reading Scripture at a pace that's equivalent to reading a newspaper or paperback novel. With *lectio divina*, Scripture is read slowly, attentively, reflecting on a single word or phrase that may be God's instruction for us. The more we engage in this type of scriptural reflection, the more we will discover how much we are able to open ourselves to an ever-intimate relationship with God, becoming more attuned to the Holy Spirit's presence in our lives.

The practice of *lectio divina*, or praying the Scriptures, involves three steps:

<u>One</u>, by sitting quietly in prayer, we ask not only for God's blessing on that time, but also for the ability to listen for the gentle whisper of Holy Spirit's voice in our hearts. First, select a passage of Scripture to read in its

entire context. It may be a story that is a paragraph or two in length, or involve two-three pages. Next, read it slowly, noting any words or phrases that grab your attention. When this occurs, do not judge how you feel or what you think about the passage.

Two, re-read the passage, interacting with the story. For example, if you're reading the passage on the Good Samaritan (Luke 10:25-37), you could place yourself in the role of the priest or Levite who passed by the beaten man. Perhaps you may imagine yourself as the one who was robbed, or the Samaritan who showed pity. If you dare, place yourself in the role of the robber and discover something else about yourself. Again, do not judge any thoughts or emotions that may emerge. Simply, make note of them.

Three, contemplate on the passage, asking God, "Where does this passage touch my life today?" Review the story in your heart and mind again and take notice of any sights, sounds, or odors that emerge. You may imagine yourself sitting by the Sea of Galilee smelling the salt air and hearing the waves crashing on the shore as Jesus delivers the Sermon on the Mount. Silently note what you see, hear or smell. Also note what emotions are stirred in you, positive and negative. For example, if a negative emotion is stirred in you as a result of reading a passage on Christ's suffering, reflect on what areas of your life are being touched. Perhaps you may be reminded about the injustices you have suffered in your life. Perhaps the story reminds you of your family or current job. At any rate, attend to how you feel as you reflect on that passage. You may even want to verbalize your feelings, such as, "When I read (hear, see, smell, etc) _____, I feel _____. Many people find it awkward at first to talk about their feelings, but the more you are able to get in touch with them, the easier it is for you to own them as parts of ourselves.

Finally, for the remainder of the time, and even throughout the rest of the day/week until your next *lectio*, reflect on what it is that God wants you to do as a result of meditating on that passage. The real transformation of *lectio divina* occurs in your lives when you act on your discoveries. They may take you in a new direction in your life. They may compel you to give up self-defeating behaviors or negative perspectives. They may urge you to examine how you interact with others, as well as how you imprison people with your attitudes of un-forgiveness and bitterness. Admittedly, you may be shocked at what you discover about yourself, or you may not be surprised at all. Regardless of your initial response, *lectio divina* will lead you to make radical changes in your life. Even if you feel as though you do not have the willingness to change at the moment, you can always ask God for the grace to begin the change in you. It is my prayer that you discover the courage to explore all that God already knows about you, yet loves you anyway.

James A. Houck, Jr., Ph.D.

He who began a good work in you will carry it to completion until the day of Christ.

Philippians 1:6

Chapter 1

I Will Make You a Real Fisherman
Luke 5:1-11, Matthew 4:18-20, Mark 1:16-18

*O*ne day as Jesus was standing by the Lake of Gennesaret, with the people crowding around him and listening to the word of God, he saw at the water's edge two boats, left there by the fishermen, who were washing their nets. He got into one of the boats, the one belonging to Simon, and asked him to put out a little from shore. Then he sat down and taught the people from the boat.

When he had finished speaking, he said to Simon, "Put out into the deep water, and let down the nets for a catch." Simon answered, "Master, we've worked hard all night and haven't caught anything. But because you say so, I will let down the nets." When they had done so, they caught such a large number of fish that their nets began to break. So they signaled their partners in the other boat to come and help *them, and they came and filled both boats so full that they began to sink.*

When Simon Peter saw this, he fell to his knees and said, "Go away from me, Lord; for I am a sinful man!" For he and all of his companions were astonished at the catch of fish they had taken, and so were James and John, the sons of Zebedee, Simon's partners. Then Jesus said to Simon, "Don't be afraid; from now on you will catch men." So they pulled their boats up on shore, left everything and followed him.

Have you ever been walking in the woods and kicked over a rock, only to discover all kinds of creepy, crawly things scurrying for cover? Of course. This is natural. Why do you think they're under there in the first place? It's cold, damp, dark and best of all it's hidden. Ironically, it's kind of like what we do with our sins. Even though we may be in a miserable place that's cold and dark, it is home to us because it's familiar. We have become so comfortable in the muck and mire that we become unnerved when our hiding spots are disturbed.

Tangney and Dearing (2002) note that shame has the potential to do a number of toxic things in us: For some people, experiencing shame causes them to run and hide. For others, shame might cause them to explode with anger or rage. Still, some people may use illicit drugs or alcohol to numb the pain. In extreme cases of shame, people have been known to commit suicide. Have you ever noticed the first thing that we do when we experience shame? We hang our heads and attempt to hide the sudden rush of redness on our cheeks. Some people sense that sinking feeling in the pit of their stomachs. Others just feel nauseated from an all too familiar feeling from childhood. From a single incident that may have occurred when we were young until now reading this story, we may have grown accustomed to walking or sitting with our heads hanging down, unable to look anyone in the eye, not to mention ourselves in the mirror. It is a feeling of being degraded, ridiculed or disgraced that keeps us from believing we can do anything of value in this life. What's worse is that we often transfer those perceptions of ourselves onto God. Perhaps unconsciously we say to ourselves, *"If people have been treating me this way all of my life, why should God be any different?"* *"I'll never be worthy enough to be in the presence of God."* *"How could God ever love a person like me?"* *"If God really knew who I am, the kinds of heinous thoughts that race through my mind, the way I've hurt people with my words, or even the way I've been hurt by others, God would want nothing to do with me, right?"* But you see, God is different. God knows everything there is to know about us: our likes, dislikes, fears, what makes us comfortable, when we feel safe, when we feel vulnerable, even our desire for power over each other. God knows all of these things about us, and more, and yet, loves us with an everlasting love (Jeremiah 31:3).

I imagine Peter felt this same way. "Who am I that you decided to come into my boat, Lord?" For Peter, there was no place to run. Perhaps that's why Jesus asked to be taken out from the shore in the first place. Since Peter couldn't get away, he cowered and begged Jesus not to come any closer to him because the light of the Lord was casting too dark of a shadow for Peter. Ironically, Jesus does comes closer, perhaps close enough to crouch down on Peter's level in order to lift him up with words of grace: *"Don't be afraid; from now on you will catch men."* Isn't it amazing how grace drives out the fear of shame and humiliation! From that moment on we are told, Peter and the rest left their boats and followed Jesus. Sixteenth century Spanish mystic John of the Cross (1542-1591) wrote:

And so the power to become sons (and daughters) of God does not come from trying with our human will to act in a godly manner. Our new birth comes as we are changed by the inward actions of grace. Grace gives us the courage, strength and boldness to let our old ways of seeing things and our past way of dealing with life be put to death. Grace opens the eyes of the soul to the high holiness and beauty and transcendent wisdom of God (in Hazard, 1994).

In the Methodist tradition, grace is foremost to understanding and appreciating one's relationship with God and others. Throughout his life, John Wesley, founder of Methodism, struggled to live faithful to God. However, he never really felt as though he measured up, let alone felt certain of his salvation. He often wondered if he was simply going through the motions of his good works without ever having the heart-felt, inward change about which he so often preached. On one hand, Wesley could identify with the unworthiness of humanity, citing a long list of shorting-comings and sins in great detail. On the other hand, he never quite saw himself in the same company as those who joyfully accepted faith in Christ as God's gift of salvation. Furthermore, he also admitted not having the sense of forgiveness that his Moravian friend Peter Bohler taught him resulted from genuine faith. Sadly, Wesley was caught between either trying to earn God's love or feeling unworthy of ever receiving it. Following a difficult and discouraging mission trip to America, he began to question his faith as never before. Then one night, something happened that forever changed his life. In 1738, at the age of 34, John Wesley attended an evening worship service in London at Aldersgate Street which moved him deeply. In his journal, Wesley described his experience:

In the evening I went very unwillingly to a society in Aldersgate Street, where one was reading Luther's preface to the Epistle to the Romans. About a quarter before nine, while the leader was describing the change which God works in the heart through faith in Christ, I felt my heart strangely warmed. I felt I did trust in Christ alone for salvation; and an assurance was given me that He had taken away my sins, even mine, and saved me from the law of sin and death (from *The Journal of John Wesley*, May 24, 1738).

From this experience, Wesley developed his theology of *prevenient, justifying* and *sanctifying grace. Prevenient grace* describes the universal work of the Holy Spirit in the hearts and lives of people between conception and conversion. Original sin, according to Wesley, made it necessary for the Holy Spirit to initiate the relationship between God and people. Bound by sin and death, people experience the gentle wooing of the Holy Spirit, which leads people to either accept or reject salvation. *Justifying grace* describes the work of the Holy Spirit at the moment of conversion in the lives of those who say "yes" to placing their faith and trust in Jesus Christ. This is what Wesley described as his *heart being strangely warmed.* Finally, *sanctifying grace* describes the work of the Holy Spirit in the lives of believers between conversion and their death. It is the on-going and progressive work of the Holy Spirit in a person, resulting in their maturing love for God and others (Hiedinger, 1986).

For us today, grace indeed is very empowering when we realize the depth of the love, acceptance and forgiveness of God. We no longer have to be afraid of being shamed or humiliated because we can walk in the light of God's grace. In fact, we can acknowledge just how damaging this fear of being humiliated is by the endless attempts of seeking approval from others in our lives. To make it sound better to us, we may call approval "affirmation." Yet, if we're honest with ourselves, it may actually be an unconscious attempt to stave off the sting of further humiliation, such as convincing ourselves that we could never be more than what we see in the mirror. However, God's grace liberates us from shame and humiliation. Like Peter in this opening chapter, this realization is only the beginning. As we shall see, Peter's willingness (and ours) to follow Jesus leads to an ever-deepening appreciation and application of this concept of grace. There's much work to be done in a person such as Peter. But then again, seeing what God can do in and through the likes of him, is why grace is called "amazing!"

Exercise:

(1) Begin by sitting comfortably. Take several deep breaths. When you are ready, read Luke 5:1-11 aloud. If you like, you may also use this exercise at another time to read aloud the words of the hymn, *"Lord, You Have Come to the Lakeshore."* Silently meditate on these words. Make a note which words resonate within your heart and soul. What sentence or phrase gets your attention? Sit with these for several minutes.

(2) As you re-read the passage, interact with the story. Reflect on the story and imagine yourself as Peter after a night of fishing. What do you hear/see/smell/feel as Jesus approaches you?

(3) Re-read the passage. Ask God, "Where does this passage touch my life today?" You may recall the times in your life when you were humiliated or felt shame by what you said or did. Remember the times when, like Peter, you also wanted to hide from Jesus. What do you feel in your heart when you realize that Jesus knows everything there is to know about you, and still loves you regardless?

(4) Finally, ask yourself, "What it is that God wants me to do as a result of meditating on this passage? Do I

withhold grace to others, as a result of my unwillingness to forgive? Who do I push away because of my sense of shame or humiliation? When I sense God in another approaching, what stance should I take? Where in my life do I need to be more open to God's grace?"

Tu Has Venido A La Orilla
(Lord, You Have Come to the Lakeshore)
Gertrude C. Suppe, George Lockwood, and Raquel Gutierrez-Achon, tr. ©1989,
The United Methodist Publishing House

Lord, you have come to the lakeshore
looking neither for wealthy nor wise ones.
You only asked me to follow humbly.

Refrain
O Lord, with your eyes you have searched me,
kindly smiling, you have spoken my name.
Now my boat's left on the shoreline behind me;
by your side I will seek other seas.

You know so well my possessions;
my boat carries no gold and no weapons;
But nets and fishes — my daily labor (refrain)

You need my hands, full of caring,

through my labors to give others rest,

and constant love that keeps on loving (refrain)

You, who have fished other oceans

ever longed-for by souls who are waiting,

my loving friend, as thus you call me.

Chapter 2

The Red Badge of Crow
Matthew 14: 22-33

*I*mmediately Jesus made the disciples get into the boat and go ahead of him to the other side, while he dismissed the crowd. After he had dismissed them, he went up on a mountainside by himself to pray. When evening came, he was there alone, but the boat was already a considerable distance from land, buffeted by the waves because the wind was against it. During the fourth watch of the night Jesus went out to them, walking on the lake. When the disciples saw him walking on the lake, they were terrified. "It's a ghost," they said, and cried out in fear. But Jesus immediately said to them, "Take courage! It is I. Don't be afraid." "Lord, if it is you," Peter replied, "Tell me to come to you on the water." "Come," he said. Then Peter got down out of the boat, walked on the water and came toward Jesus. But when he saw the wind, he was afraid and, beginning to sink, cried out, "Lord, save*

me!" Immediately Jesus reached out his hand and caught him. "You of little faith," he said, "why did you doubt?" And when he climbed into the boat, the wind died down. Then those who were in the boat worshiped him saying, "Truly you are the Son of God."

We all can identify with being caught up in a moment of passion, danger or excitement.

Depending on the circumstance, we might feel invincible, bulletproof and rugged when the adrenaline is surging, our hearts pumping and our breathing fast and shallow. Concurrently, our minds are racing as all neurological synapses are firing away at an alarming rate. For the most part, this normal physiological reaction occurs when we are faced with either a dangerous or thrilling situation. This wave of exhiliation is so great for some people that they never want it to end, hence the name "adrenaline junkie." In fact, many may engage in dangerous or stressful activities just for the adrenaline rush. For example, a sky-diver may feed off of the rush he or she receives by defying the laws of gravity before the parachute opens. Stage performers may be thrilled at the applause and cheers they receive from the audience. Whatever the situation, the thrill will come to an end. It has to. Otherwise, our immune system will be compromised because our bodies are not meant to sustain that kind of physiological surge for long periods of time. Moreover, when we calm down and are able to reflect on our experiences, we may realize how quickly we overlooked the potential for harm, as well as how close we may have come to hurting ourselves and others. We may even catch ourselves saying, "What was I thinking?" In another example, some people are unable to tolerate the quiet and the let down following a command performance on a sports field or in a theater. In the stillness of the air, their minds may already be looking ahead to the next big thrill just so they can feel that rush again. However, in that moment they realize that like Napoleon, *"all glory is fleeting."*

Stephen Crane once wrote about such a young man named Henry in the *Red Badge of Courage*. Henry was only 15 years old when he joined the Union Army in the Civil War. For this young man, the stories of valor, the sound of warfare, the smell of smoke and the thrill of victory, were all enticing. However, it was not long before the horrors of war put a bad taste in his mouth. During one battle Henry felt his courage quickly drain away he fled the advancing army with its canons and rifles. Afterwards, he justified his retreat by convincing himself that saving his own neck was a good thing. Still, Henry received his "red badge" for valor, although not from surviving a fierce battle, but from an accidental injury. Another fleeing soldier knocked him on the head with his rifle. His "wound" transforms into his badge of courage in the eyes of others, but to himself, he knows there was much more to the story. If they only knew the whole truth! His friend Wilson leads Henry back to the regiment and cares for him as he believes Henry was shot. In the days that follow, Henry fights courageously on the battlefield, unleashing all of his pent-up aggression and frustration. Following one final battle, Henry reflects on his experiences in the war. Though he revels in his success, he feels deeply ashamed of his behavior; especially the times when he watched his friends die.

Henry wasn't the only one enthralled with glory on the battlefield. Both Francis of Assisi (1182-1226) and Ignatius of Loyola (1491-1556), who later went on to become influential spiritual leaders and join the rank of canonized saints, initially sought that kind of fame. Francis wanted to be a knight and believed that the thick of battle was the best place for the glory and prestige for which he longed. However, when Assisi declared war on Perugia, Francis was taken prisoner. A year later he was released, searching for his glory. When the call to arms came again during the Fourth Crusade (1199-1204), Francis followed the call but never saw one battle. After being visited by God in a dream, Francis returned home to begin his service to the poor and the marginalized.

Centuries later, another soldier Ignatius of Loyola was critically wounded when a cannonball shattered one of his legs during a French assault on the ramparts of Pamplona.

During the many months of recovery, Ignatius documented his conversion experience in letters, an autobiography and a guided retreat he called his Spiritual Exercises, the foundation of Ignatian spirituality. When he was able to walk again, Ignatius spent nearly a year in the mountain town of Manresa, helping nuns care for the sick in a local hospital. When he wasn't helping the sick, Ignatius withdrew to a small cave to meditate and do severe penance for his past sins. The rule of his "band of brothers," the Society of Jesus or Jesuits captures many of the charisms of the soldier, but in their case they are soldiers of Christ, defenders of God's will.

In my life, I've met many veterans of wars who had won service medals and ribbons for their battlefield virtues such as leadership and valor. They all had their stories to tell about the kind of hell-on-earth they went through and survived. Yet in spite of how many stories they told, there was always a sobering thread that tied each of those memories together: They all knew deep down inside that while one day a person might be considered brave, on any other day, he or she just might be lucky. In other words, the glorious tales of war are more often left to those who write novels and make movies.

I imagine this is how Peter must have felt when he saw Jesus walking on the water. It must have been some sight! I'm convinced Peter had no doubt in Jesus' capabilities; he just doubted his own ability to hold on and believe no matter how illogical the circumstances. In his fear and self-doubt, he looked away from Christ. Many times we too are guilty of "taking our eyes off of Jesus" and focusing on the problems at hand. This is a very easy thing to do, especially if we see no way out of a difficult circumstance. While in at-risk situations we have to realize the danger to others and ourselves that is involved, we don't need to live in a state of denial of our problems. Neither do we need to swing to the other perspective of total gloom. The real lesson here is for us to stay focused on Christ regardless of how much the wind is blowing.

Proverbs 16:18 says, *"Pride goes before destruction, a haughty spirit before a fall."* We read this passage but may be tempted to think that it only applies to others; after all, a little bragging isn't so bad, right? I hope you're hungry, because nobody likes to eat crow. Crows are not noted as being a delicacy in restaurants. I've never seen them on the menu, and as scavengers, these birds are not fit to eat. The expression, "to eat crow" means to suffer embarrassment by having to admit your mistake. Another way to understand this phrase is to think of it as the necessity to retract an earlier statement. Often this kind of embarrassment is the result of having made some outlandish claim, one that stretches far outside the bounds of reality. Afterward the crow eating, you realize that you're human just like everybody else. Bon appetite!

Perhaps it's human to think we're often larger than life itself. The mental health field refers to this kind of thinking, when it is taken to the extreme, as *delusions of the grandiose type.* The problem is that with people who have this diagnosis, eating crow is not on the menu. Caught in their delusional world, it is very difficult to convince them they are wrong. Usually, it takes several people who not only point out the erroneous perceptions, but also reinforce what is real. That, and the right prescription medication helps too. However, in all fairness to Peter, he was the only one of the disciples to get out of the boat and go toward Jesus. Peter proved himself a man of his word. . . just not a man who understood the limitations of his faith. Wisdom is a combination of two elements: life experience and learning from mistakes. Live long enough to reflect on your mistakes and hopefully wisdom will be produced. The people who are the wisest ones are those who can learn from the mistakes of others.

We all face circumstances for which we are not prepared. Each day is different and brings different challenges. In fact, we may never be in a similar position to Peter, but we can learn from him. The truth we can inculcate in ourselves is that despite our daily challenges one thing remains consistent; namely, the presence of Christ. As I tell my counseling students, "Never underestimate the value of presence!"

A tiny detail that is often overlooked in this passage is the phrase from Matthew spoken by Jesus is, *"Take courage! It is I. Don't be afraid."* In its basic expression it can simply be put,"Fear not!" This phrase, in various combinations, is mentioned approximately 64 times in the Bible, and always in the context of God doing something new. For example, what did God first tell Joshua when he was about to besiege the city of Ai? *"Fear not, neither be dismayed."* (Joshua 10:8) How did the prophet Isaiah assure the Israelites that God had not forgotten them in their time of exile? *"Fear not, for I am with you."* (Seven times between Isaiah 41-44) In the gospels, what did the angels first say to the shepherds when they announced the birth of Jesus? *"Fear not, for behold I bring you glad tidings of great joy!"* (Luke 2:10) The words echo on and on and on. Every time God was bringing about change, or was about to do something that had never been seen or heard of before, "Fear not" began the sentence. Why? Why are people first told not to be afraid? Quite simply, because fear immobilizes us. Fear keeps us in the boat where we feel safe, surrounded by our familiar and predictable environment.

It's normal to feel afraid in the midst of something new and different, but fear does not encourage us to step out in faith. Despite taking his eyes off of Jesus in the storm, Peter learned a valuable lesson: Jesus never took his eyes off Peter. This paradox reminds me of a story that tells that one night a house caught fire and a young boy was trapped on the roof. The father stood on the ground below with outstretched arms, calling to his son, "Jump! I'll catch you." He knew the boy had to jump to save his life. All the boy could see, however, was flame, smoke, and blackness. Terrified, he was paralyzed, afraid to leave the roof. His father kept yelling: "Jump! I will catch you." The boy shouted, "Daddy, I can't see you." The father replied, "That's ok, I can see you." The presence of Christ is always with us, encouraging perseverance of faith. Perhaps Peter was reminded of this experience when he later wrote in his first epistle:

In this you greatly rejoice, though now for a little while you may have had to suffer grief in all kinds of trials. These have come so that your faith—of greater worth than gold, which perishes even though refined by fire—may be proved genuine and may result in praise, glory and honor when Jesus Christ is revealed. Though you have not seen him, you love him; and even though you do not see him now, you believe in him and are filled with an inexpressible and glorious joy, for you are receiving the goal of your faith, the salvation of your souls (1 Peter 1:6-9)

There's a familiar story about a painter who wanted to capture the essence of absolute peace on canvas, so he decided to paint a picture of the fiercest storm he could. The background sky was horrifying with its ominous black clouds, with streaks of lightening flashing across the horizon. The waves swelled and crashed with fury against the jagged rocks on the shore. If you closed your eyes you could almost feel the stinging rains against your face. As you look closely at the painting, you can notice off in the corner a mother seagull with her chicks nestled quietly under some rocks. How serene she sits there; content to ignore the fierce storm raging around them. To the painter, this is the face of peace. For the rest of us, the lesson of wisdom is that peace is found not is not the absence of life's storms; peace is that inner stillness in the midst of the worst of weather's fury. Jesus says: "Take heart, it is I; do not be afraid." No matter what the storms, no matter what the trials, Jesus is always there for us.

Exercise:

(1) Begin by sitting comfortably. Take several deep breaths. When you are ready, read Matthew 14:22-33 aloud. If you like, you may also use this exercise to read aloud the words of the hymn, "Rock of Ages." Silently meditate on the words. Make a note, which words resonate within your heart and soul. What sentence or phrase gets your attention? Sit with these for several minutes.

(2) As you re-read the passage, interact with the story. Reflect on the story and imagine yourself as Peter watching Jesus walk across the water. What do you hear/

see/smell/feel as Jesus approaches you? What comes to mind when you hear Jesus say, "Fear not!"

(3) Re-read the passage. Ask God, "Where does this passage touch my life today?" You may recall the times in your life when your fears paralyzed you from making decisions. Remember a time when, like Peter, you initially trusted Jesus, then became disheartened when you focused you attention on the circumstances or obstacles that were in the way. What do you feel in your heart when you realize that Jesus knows your deepest fears and still calls for you to reach out to him in trust?

(4) Finally, ask yourself, "What it is that God wants me to do as a result of meditating on this passage?" "Is there an area in my life that I need to trust God more with?" "How can I assure others of peace in the midst of their storms of life?"

Rock of Ages

Words by Augustus M. Toplady, 1740-1778

Music by Thomas Hastings, 1784-1872

Rock of Ages, cleft for me,
Let me hide myself in Thee.
Let the water and the blood,
From Thy wounded side which flowed,
Be of sin the double cure,
Save from wrath and make me pure.

Nothing in my hand I bring,
Simply to Thy cross I cling;
Naked come to Thee for dress,
Helpless look to Thee for grace;
Foul I to the fountain fly,
Wash me Savior or I die.

Not the labor of my hands,
Can fulfill Thy law's demands;
Could my zeal no respite know,
Could my tears forever flow,
All for sin could not atone;
Thou must save and Thou alone.

While I draw this fleeting breath,
When my eyes shall close in death,
When I rise to worlds unknown,
And behold Thee on Thy throne,
Rock of Ages cleft for me,
Let me hide myself in Thee.

Could my tears forever flow?
Could my zeal no languor know?
These for sin could not atone;
Thou must save, and Thou alone.
In my hand no price I bring;
Simply to thy cross I cling.

Chapter 3

"More Information, Please!"
Matthew 15:10-20

*J*esus called the crowd to him and said, *"Listen and understand. What goes into a man's mouth does not make him 'unclean,' but what comes out of his mouth, that is what makes him unclean." Then the disciples came to him and asked, "Do you know that the Pharisees were offended when they heard this?" He replied, "Every plant that my heavenly Father has not planted will be pulled up by the roots. Leave them; they are blind guides. If a blind man leads a blind man, both will fall into a pit." Peter said, "Explain the parable to us." "Are you still so dull?" Jesus asked them. "Don't you see that whatever enters the mouth goes into the stomach and then out of the body? But the things that come out of the mouth come from the heart, and these make a man 'unclean.' For out of the heart come evil thoughts, murder, adultery, sexual immorality, theft, false testimony, slander. These are*

what make a man 'unclean'; but eating with unwashed hands does not make him 'unclean.'

I'm sure we've all heard the saying, "There's no such thing as a stupid question." Comforting as that may be for us, I'm also sure that there have been times we simply wished we hadn't asked the question we did? It's not that we believed we asked a stupid question to which there was an overtly obvious answer. Rather the answer we received was certainly more than what we bargained for. In this chapter, I'm convinced Peter wanted to make sure he was getting it right. He had been on this journey with Jesus for some time now, and he's starting to put things together. Of course, he wanted to know exactly what he needed to do in order to find favor with God. Who doesn't? We all want to have that assurance that what we are doing is pleasing to God. This is natural. What's even better is if we could point to something externally in our lives in order to demonstrate our faithfulness before God and others (such as bragging about what and how much we do). It would be better, that is, if you are a Pharisee.

For the most part, the Pharisees were very passionate about keeping the Law of Moses. In fact, we might say that they were downright fanatical in their devotion to God. They were truly experts at knowing what to do and what not to do. They knew how much and how often one needed to perform in order to be pleasing to God. Unfortunately, in their efforts to find favor they totally ignored the spirit of the law. They focused solely on outward appearances of holiness instead of possessing the inner transformation of having God's laws "written on their hearts." (Jeremiah 31:33) For example, in Matthew 12:1-14, Jesus and his disciples were walking through a grain field, picking some kernels and eating them. The Pharisees who saw this were upset because they said this was an "unlawful" thing to do on the Sabbath. Ironically, their problem was not that Jesus and his disciples were eating grain on the Sabbath, but rather the Pharisees interpreted picking and eating the kernels from a field as the same thing as "harvesting and threshing" grain. That type of manual labor was clearly forbidden on the Sabbath as spelled out in the Mosaic law. Nevertheless, the Pharisee's legal adherence to the letter of the law had prevented them from being open to a more spiritual understanding and freedom in everyday life.

Now before we criticize the Pharisees too much, we need to realize that they had the best intentions in serving God they way they did. Long before the Pharisees came into the world, their ancestors were exiled to Assyria (730-710 B.C) and Babylon (597-581 B.C.) as a result of their disobedience to God. However, prior to these exiles, God sent prophets to call the people to repent from their wickedness or else suffer God's impending judgment for their continued disregard of the Covenant and worshiping foreign gods. Despite these prophetic interventions, the Israelites persisted in their wickedness, and the armies from Assyria and Babylon eventually attacked and carried away thousands of Israelites from the land God had promised to them. After many years in foreign captivity, the people eventually returned to Israel to rebuild their lives. From that point on, younger generations were taught to heed the mistakes of their ancestors. By the time of Jesus, the Pharisees emerged as the ruling class responsible for maintaining holiness unto God. Since they were so fearful of breaking their covenant relationship with God, they established psuedo-laws (such as interpreting picking grain on the Sabbath as work) to avoid coming close to breaking God's original law (you shall do no work on the Sabbath).

The Pharisees also applied their interpretation to their observance of the purity laws in Leviticus. According to the Mosaic Law, there were certain kinds of foods the Israelites were forbidden to eat. Consuming certain kinds of foods as well as coming in contact with various aspects of life and/or diseases, rendered a person ceremonially unclean. This condition meant that the person was excluded from the Israelite community for a certain period of time until their physical condition improved or enough time had elapsed, whereby the person would be pronounced "clean," and be permitted to return to the community. Leviticus 11-

15 provides a complete list of clean and unclean foods and practices. Again, by the time of Jesus, the Pharisees made the consequences for being ceremonially unclean permanent as people were forced to live in seclusion, such as leper colonies.

Throughout history, certain diseases have also carried a social stigma and have often struck fear and contempt into the hearts and lives of people around the world. Whether it was leprosy in early biblical times, tuberculosis (phthisis) in Ancient Greece, the Bubonic Plague in the Middle Ages, or the Acquired Immune Deficiency Syndrome (AIDS) in the late-twentieth century, societies have displayed a pattern of purposefully disenfranchising people who contracted these diseases. Initially, this reaction was justified as necessary in order to prevent the further spread of communicable diseases. However, many afflicted people interpreted being quarantined as society's way of displaying contempt for its sick, and in some cases, they were correct. As a result, many felt stigmatized by their illness, shunned, and alienated from fully participating in their communities as persons of value and worth.

Goffman (1986) notes that the Greeks originated the term "stigma" to refer to bodily signs, designed to expose something unusual and negative about the moral status of the bearer. These "signs," imposed by society, were cut or burned into a person's body, advertising his/her condition, i.e., a slave, a criminal, or a traitor. As a result, this act of "branding" signified to all that the recipient was a blemished person, ritually polluted, and to be avoided. . .especially in public places. Such "markings" not only spoiled a person's social identity but also cut that person off from society, forcing him/her to live in isolation in an un-accepting world. From this aspect, it appeared as though there was no way to remove this outward sign, let alone recover from the emotional wounding from such harsh treatment.

This was not always the case. According to the Ancient Israelite purity laws, a distinction was made between the holy and the profane, or between the clean and unclean. As Wenham (1979) notes, cleanliness is the normal condition of most things and persons. Anything else, e.g., death, sickness, diseases, coming into contact with blood, etc., was considered a deviation from the norm, and the carrier was separated for a period of time from the community to avoid further contamination. For example, certain persistent skin diseases, among which is what is today called leprosy, were viewed as especially destructive and their symptoms, repugnant, and thus a variation from a normal skin condition. Consequently, the leprous person was expelled from the community for the duration of his/her illness. If the patient returned to normal, the person would be readmitted to the community by having the priest pronounce him/her "clean." Specific sacrifices were then offered to complete the ritual of purification

(Wenham, 1979). Although this purity system was meant to impose "temporary" isolation, the practice eventually became an acceptable way to expel people permanently, who "polluted" society by their conditions (Black, 1996). This expulsion was true not only for people who had an identifiable condition but also for those who had a condition that was not readily seen, such as mental illness.

In the context of Matthew 15, Jesus explained to his disciples that the true difference between being clean or unclean is actually a matter of the heart and not the stomach. In other words, true holiness is not based on what you take into your intestines, but rather what you take into your heart. Either way, what goes in will come out. However, the Pharisees' legalism to these purity laws did not allow them to hear the spiritual emphasis of Jesus' words. All they were concerned about was avoiding punishment from God for their lack of obedience. For us, it's always a good practice to reflect on our lives on a regular basis. We need to examine our motivations, relationships, how we are being true to our feelings and how we treat others. Is our spiritual life motivated by the love of God and a desire to get to know Him more intimately, or are we motivated out of a sense of fear of punishment? Is what we do intended to keep God from coming too close? Admittedly, we all have unwritten purity laws within our hearts. We decide in a nano-second who's "clean" or "unclean" by outward appearances. We decide in a blink of an eye who is acceptable in our society and who is not. In fact, there may have been times when we even act like a Pharisee, keeping at a distance people who challenge our understanding of God. Perhaps we are like Peter, realizing that we have to let go of some of our preconceived ideas about who we want God to be for us in order to grow in our faith.

Exercise:

(1) Begin by sitting comfortably. Take several deep breaths. When you are ready, read Matthew 15:10-20, or Psalm 51, aloud. Make a note, which words resonate within your heart and soul. What sentence or phrase gets your attention? Sit with these for several minutes.

(2) As you re-read the passage, interact with the story. Reflect on the story and imagine yourself as Peter listening to Jesus explaining this parable. Imagine yourself as one of the Pharisees and what do you hear/see/smell/feel as Jesus reproaches you?

(3) Re-read the passage. Ask God, "Where does this passage touch my life today?" Who are the people in society you consider "clean or unclean?" How do your own unclean thoughts and motivations sabotage your relationship

with God and others? What do you feel in your heart when you realize that Jesus knows your inmost thoughts, yet loves you anyway?

(4) Finally, ask yourself, "What it is that God wants me to do as a result of meditating on this passage?" "What areas of my life do I need to probe the depth of God's love more for myself and in my relationships?"

Psalm 51

Have mercy on me, O God,
according to your unfailing love;
according to your great compassion blot out my
transgressions. Wash away all my iniquity and
cleanse me from my sin.

For I know my transgressions, and my sin is always before
me. Against you, you only, have I sinned and done
what is evil in your sight,
so that you are proven right when you speak
and justified when you judge.

Surely I was sinful at birth, sinful from the time my mother
conceived me. Surely you desire truth in the inner parts;
you teach me wisdom in the inmost place.

*Cleanse me with hyssop, and I will be clean; wash me, and
I will be whiter than snow. Let me hear joy and gladness;
let the bones you have crushed rejoice. Hide your face
from my sins and blot out all my iniquity.*

*Create in me a pure heart, O God, and renew a steadfast
spirit within me. Do not cast me from your presence or take
your Holy Spirit from me. Restore to me the joy of your
salvation and grant me a willing spirit, to sustain me.*

*Then I will teach transgressors your ways, and sinners
will turn back to you. Save me from bloodguilt, O God,
the God who saves me, and my tongue will sing of your
righteousness. O Lord, open my lips, and my mouth
will declare your praise.*

*You do not delight in sacrifice, or I would bring it; you do
not take pleasure in burnt offerings. The sacrifices of God
are a broken spirit; a broken and contrite heart,
O God, you will not despise.*

*In your good pleasure make Zion prosper; build up the
walls of Jerusalem. Then there will be righteous sacrifices,
whole burnt offerings to delight you;
then bulls will be offered on your altar.*

Chapter 4

"Finally, Got This One Right!"
Matthew 16:13-20, Mark 7:27-30, Luke 9:18-21

*W*hen *Jesus came to the region of Caesarea Phillipi,*
he asked his disciples, "Who do people say the
Son of Man is?" They replied, "Some say John the Baptist;
others say Elijah; and still others say Jeremiah or one of
the prophets." "But what about you?" he asked, "Who do
you say that I am?" Simon Peter answered, "You are the
Christ, the Son of the living God!" Jesus replied, "Blessed
are you Simon son of Jonah, for this was not revealed to you
by man, but by my Father in heaven. And I tell you that you
are Peter, and on this rock I will build my church, and the
gates of Hades will not overcome it. I will give you the keys
of the kingdom of heaven; whatever you bind on earth will
be bound in heaven; and whatever you loose on earth will be
loosed in heaven." Then he warned his disciples not to tell
anyone that he was the Christ.

If you have ever played along at home with people who are on those TV game-shows, you probably know how Peter felt after giving the correct answer. Imagine, everybody is sitting around the television with puzzled looks on their faces, scratching their heads for the right answer to a piece of trivia. Then, all of a sudden the light bulb goes off in your head and you shout out the correct response! Everybody is amazed, including you, as to how you came up with that answer. Now imagine playing that game with the disciples. This time, not only does Jesus tell you that you answered correctly, but you also won the grand prize: He has chosen you to be the one through whom he can build his church! Way to go, Peter!

Isn't it nice to have somebody acknowledge you for your ideas, your thoughts, your ambitions, etc.? To have others affirm you that you're on the right track? However, we are not talking about discovering the hidden pieces to life's puzzle. Instead, we are talking about conviction. Conviction is a belief in something or someone with absolute certainty. It invokes strong emotions in us because we are often very passionate about what we believe. In religious terms we call this faith. Hebrews 11:1 says, *"Now faith is being sure of what we hope for and certain of what we do not see."* Although this is a familiar passage quoted by Christians during difficult times, faith should never be reduced to merely a mental coping exercise whereby we can perhaps convince ourselves that we will make it through a difficult time in our lives if we reiterate that to ourselves enough. While it is true that our beliefs do sustain us, most people often neglect the other side of faith; namely, action. Faith is just as much a verb as it is a noun. What we believe, as well as the extent of what we believe, will govern our actions sooner or later.

This all sounds so simple, yet I can't tell you how many times I have counseled people who struggle with finding the *assurance of their faith*. They either vacillate between shame (I am flawed), or feelings of guilt (I did something wrong). Either way, faith is something that for they yearn for more. Elizabeth was such a person. A woman in her mid-fifties, she came to me for counseling to treat her anxiety attacks. Elizabeth's main concern was, "Why would a devout Christian struggle with anxiety? After all, I shouldn't be feeling this way if I had enough faith, right?" She would often comment how she was a faithful wife and mother to her family. By all outward appearances Elizabeth had all the virtues needed to be a spiritual mentor to others. The only problem was that when it came to perfectionism, Elizabeth was "off the charts!" She was meticulous in everything she did. She had an careful eye for detail and a razor sharp pencil to make "to-do lists." However, Elizabeth lived in fear that what she did was never good enough. Behind all of her good works lingered the dread that if she stopped being busy, she would fall out of favor with God. This fear of displeasing God haunted her during her waking and sleeping hours, until it started to take its toll on her physically and emotionally. In our first session together, Elizabeth looked haggard and worn out despite her neat and tidy appearance. She asked me, *"How do you know you've done enough for God?"* Obviously, this was her life-long question, one which reflected her lack of understanding of grace. I did not find this surprising, because it has been my experience that when people wrestle with whether or not they are doing, or have done, enough for God, they also typically find the message of grace difficult to grasp.

John Wesley also struggled with the concept of grace in his early life. Following a disappointing evangelistic ministry in America, John returned home extremely disappointed. He wrote, *"I went to America to convert Indians; but oh, who shall convert me?"* Despite his education, devotion and service to God, Wesley had no peace in his heart. On the voyage back to England, Wesley sailed with Moravians, a group of devoted Christians. During a severe storm at sea, the Moravians sang and praised God, despite the storm. What astonished Wesley was that he saw they were at peace. Instead, Wesley quietly wrote about his terror and fear of death. He wasn't sure about whether or not he was accepted by God. The bravery and confidence of the Moravians convinced Wesley they had something he didn't have. They knew they were secure and safe with God, while

Wesley merely hoped he was saved. The Moravians asked him, *"Do you know you are a child of God? Does the Spirit of God bear witness with your spirit that you are a child of God?"* No one ever asked Wesley that before. By all outward appearances, everyone assumed he was a Christian. Wesley didn't have an answer. The Moravians continued, *"Do you know Jesus Christ?"* Wesley hesitated for a moment, then answered, *"I know He is the Savior of the world."* *"True,"* replied the Moravians, *"but do you know He has saved YOU?"* Wesley, still confused, could only say *"I hope He died to save me."* Wesley knew he lacked conviction behind these words. From that moment on Wesley eventually found the grace he was searching for at his Aldersgate experience and preached ferverently on God's grace and the assurance of every believer's salvation in Christ. He later wrote, *"It pleased God to kindle a fire, which I trust shall never be extinguished."*

Grace (*charis* in biblical Greek), in its simplest terms, means to find favor with God. It is not based on what we have done or can do, but based on God's love for us. Grace differs from mercy in that mercy is something a person receives in the place of deserved punishment. While grace implies receiving an undeserved positive benefit, such as finding inner strength during difficult times or overcoming personal limitations, the sense of punishment is not involved. In Christian circles, grace is understood as the divine gift of salvation given by God through Christ which is accepted by faith (Ephesians 2:8). Moreoever, there is no way we could ever atone for our sins; there are just too many of them, along with our sinful nature. Despite our best efforts to remove our sinfulness, the stain of our sins would forever remain in our hearts. Just like an old, stubborn stain that has permanently ruined a favorite shirt, so too is the stain of our iniquity. This insight is the major difference between the Old Testament animal sacrifices and Jesus' death on the cross and resurrection in the gospels. As Hebrews 10:1-14 puts it:

The law is only a shadow of the good things that are coming—not the realities themselves. For this reason it can never, by the same sacrifices repeated endlessly year after year, make perfect those who draw near to worship. If it could, would they not have stopped being offered? For the worshipers would have been cleansed once for all, and would no longer have felt guilty for their sins. But those sacrifices are an annual reminder of sins, because it is impossible for the blood of bulls and goats to take away sins. Therefore, when Christ came into the world, he said: "Sacrifice and offering you did not desire, but a body you prepared for me; with burnt offerings and sin offerings you were not pleased."

Then I said, 'Here I am—it is written about me in the scroll— I have come to do your will, O God.' First he said,

"Sacrifices and offerings, burnt offerings and sin offerings you did not desire, nor were you pleased with them" (although the law required them to be made). Then he said, "Here I am, I have come to do your will." He sets aside the first to establish the second. And by that will, we have been made holy through the sacrifice of the body of Jesus Christ once for all.

Day after day every priest stands and performs his religious duties; again and again he offers the same sacrifices, which can never take away sins. But when this priest had offered for all time one sacrifice for sins, he sat down at the right hand of God. Since that time he waits for his enemies to be made his footstool, because by one sacrifice he has made perfect forever those who are being made holy.

This is not to say that grace was not available to people in Old Testament times. Indeed the sacrificial offerings mentioned in Leviticus permitted the priests to sacrifice animals and use their blood as a covering for people's sins. Although the people's sins were atoned for, the guilt of their consciences remained because the blood of animals was merely a substitute for their sins. Still, they offered their sacrifices by faith, looking ahead to the time when God would someday provide a permanent sacrifice that would remove sin and guilt completely. Jesus' life and blood provided this complete atonement on our behalf when he offered his life and blood completely at Calvary.

On a daily basis, it is through the grace that God imparts to us that we find the strength we need in times of trouble, hope in the midst of despair, forgiveness in place of sin, healing in the place of pain and suffering. Admittedly, grace is difficult to conceive at times. In fact, more often than not, we recognize those grace moments in our lives in hindsight. This was something Elizabeth needed to understand. Peter too. Despite Peter's conviction Jesus does not give Peter a millisecond to beam, but rather puts his answer into a spiritual context: This was divine revelation! The only reason Peter could say what he did with conviction was that God revealed to him that Jesus was the Christ, the Anointed, Holy One of God. Little did Peter realize that he would need grace throughout the rest of his life. Not only would he recognize that in Jesus was the fulfillment of divine grace for the forgiveness of his sins, but also that it carried the transformative and sustaining power of the Holy Spirit that he would need in order to do the work of God.

For Elizabeth, embracing grace in her life was indeed a challenge. To understand that grace is indeed a gift from God, she needed to look beyond the terms of salvation Christ offers, to the moment to moment events in our day. Elizabeth needed to begin by looking at her motivation. Why did she do the things she did, not in terms of quantity but rather quality. Instead of listing everything she did for others to meet an unconscious quota, she needed to examine the quality of physical, emotional and spiritual needs being met. Together, we looked at her gift of giving and service. It was all about her. *"Have I done enough?" "Will others recognize what I have done for them?"* Underneath it all was a strong motivation of co-dependency which focused on her needs being met (alleviation of guilt), rather than focusing on the needs of others. When she perceived her efforts weren't being appreciated, she became anxious and sought to do more to deal with her anxiety. However, by embracing God's grace she recognized that her giving was perhaps God's way of using her as an instrument of grace for others. Therefore, she did not need to worry about whether or not she was doing enough for God? The question then became whether or not she could serve others in humility, by removing everything that hinders (namely herself) God's grace, by stepping aside and allowing God's grace to flow through her service? I knew she had taken a huge step when she realized, *"You know what? It's not about me, is it? It's about what God can do in me and through me. I just need to get out of the way!"* Bravo!

Spiritual growth through humility and service is not a numbers game, something we can hold up to God as a sign of our faithfulness. Instead, we need to hold those deeds up as a sign of God's faithfulness to us. We will be tempted to keep track of our good works as if we're holding an ace up our sleeves, the chips of our good, righteous service. But truth be told, the ace we have is found in Christ and Christ alone. All glory, honor and praise are his because of the on-going transformation occurring in our lives through the work of the Holy Spirit. May we have the full assurance of faith in God to be able to complete the work that Christ has begun in us, and carrying it through to others, unto the glory of God!

Exercise:

(1) Begin by sitting comfortably. Take several deep breaths. When you are ready, read Matthew 16:13-20, Mark 7:27-30, or Luke 9:18-21 aloud. Silently meditate on these words. Make a note, which words resonate within your heart and soul. What sentence or phrase gets your attention? Sit with these for several minutes. You may also want to read Hebrews 10:22-23:

Draw near to God with a sincere heart in full assurance of faith, having our hearts sprinkled to cleanse us from a guilty conscious and having our bodies washed with pure water. Let us hold unswervingly to the hope that we profess, for he who promised is faithful.

(2) As you re-read the passage, interact with the story. Reflect on the story and imagine yourself as one of the disciples watching Peter discover this divine revelation. Share in his excitement. Where do the words, "You are the Christ!" impact to you? In what ways (subtle and otherwise) has God revealed His truth to you? How do your convictions influence your faith and actions?

(3) Re-read the passage. Ask God, "Where does this passage touch my life today?" "How does grace impact my life?" "How does my understanding of grace impact your relationships with others?" "What keeps me from being a vessel of grace for others?" What do you feel in your heart when you realize that Jesus' death and resurrection was God's chosen method to impart grace and forgiveness to you?

(4) Finally, ask yourself, "What it is that God wants me to do as a result of meditating on this passage?" "How would my life change if I fully embraced the assurance of God's forgiveness, salvation and love?" "How different would my life look like to myself and others if I fully embraced God's grace?"

Chapter 5

"Quit While You're Ahead!"
Matthew 16:21-28, Mark 8:31-9:1

*F*rom that time Jesus began to explain to his disciples that he must go to Jerusalem and suffer many things at the hands of the elders, chief priests, and teachers of the law, and that he must be killed and on the third day be raised to life. Peter took him aside and began to rebuke him. "Never, Lord!" he said, "This shall never happen to you!" Jesus turned and said to Peter, "Get behind me, Satan! You are a stumbling block to me; you do not have in mind the things of God, but the things of men." Then Jesus said to his disciples, "If anyone would come after me, he must deny himself and take up his cross and follow me. For whoever wants to save his life will lose it, but whoever loses his life for me will find it. What good will it be for a man if he gains the whole world, yet forfeit his soul? Or what can a man give in exchange for his soul? For the Son of Man is going to come in his Father's*

glory with his angels, and then he will reward each person according to what he has done. I tell you the truth, some of you standing here will not taste death before they see the Son of Man coming in his kingdom.

When you were younger, did you ever wish you had a magic lamp? Come on, admit it. What! You never fantasized about finding some old, rusty oil lamp somewhere in a garbage heap? You give it a couple of rubs with your hands and "poof!" Out comes a beautiful genie, ready to grant you your heart's desire. You are awestruck as your mind immediately begins to race with all the possibilities of what to wish for. Would you wish for world peace? Would you ask for enough money for yourself and your family? What about fame and recognition? Perhaps the genie would equip you with the skills to help others develop their own gifts? Yes, the possibilities are endless! Yet ironically, when you boil down this scenario, the real fantasy of having a genie in your back pocket is the belief that you are in control of your life. You feel empowered to make decisions that will put you in charge. Perhaps for once in your life you are the one who calls the shots instead of having to follow another person's direction for you.

As outrageous as this story sounds, how many times are we guilty of reducing God to being the genie in the lamp? Instead of having an open, on-going devotion with God, we keep Him locked away where He is safe, perhaps from us, and then allow God to be released only to grant us what we need or want. Afterwards, we demand God go back inside the lamp until another day. Interestingly, by keeping God under wraps in this manner, we live under the illusion that God conforms to our expectations and plays by our rules. Unfortunately, this kind of behavior is all too common in today's Christianity. I have counseled many people who come to crisis moments in their faith simply because God did not live up to their expectations. For some people, God didn't answer their prayers according to their specifics, or God's answer to prayer wasn't fast enough, or they were convinced God misunderstood their prayer requests. Regardless, a preconceived idea of who God is and how God should behave (or should I say, how we hope God behaves), often does not match the circumstances.

For Peter, this rebuke from Jesus must have been quite a shock! Imagine, one minute Jesus tells him that he's the rock upon which the Church will be built. Then in the next breath when Peter makes a mistake, he is described as a stumbling block. Which image is correct? After all, things were going so great up to this point. Oh Peter had a few "oops" moments and embarrassing situations, but for the most part, he was starting to catch on. It seemed as if everything was falling into place like the pieces of a puzzle fitting together. In fact,

I believe Peter was beginning to see himself as part of this puzzle too.

I imagine this exchange with Jesus must have tapped into quite a few emotional changes in Peter, changes that ranged from being startled and humiliated perhaps even to embarrassed and confused. However, what Peter needed to learn was that the Church would not be built with wood, stone and mortar, but would be built upon the suffering, death and resurrection of Jesus Christ. Peter's role in this birth of the early church depended on his own life's transformation through Jesus' death on the cross and resurrection. Jesus quickly corrects Peter's (and perhaps our) misperceptions of who he is and what he has come to do. Furthermore, instead of adhering to the expectations of what others believed the Messiah to be (*who do others say that I am?*), Jesus emphatically spells out his expectations of what true discipleship is: self-denial, taking up one's cross, and following him.

Following the way Jesus had chosen through the cross was indeed radically different from what the people were expecting a triumphant Messiah to do. They believed Jesus would lead the overthrow of the Roman Empire and set the Israelites free once and for all. However, by embracing his suffering, crucifixion, and resurrection, Jesus' focused on a greater freedom from sin and death (Galatians 5:1) that called for a total commitment from all followers. Therefore, self-denial, taking up one's cross, and following Jesus is not a part-time venture, or whenever it is convenient for us.

To follow Jesus means that we also surrender any self-promoting behaviors. For example, humility is quickly becoming a lost characteristic in today's Christianity. Instead of seeing humility as the strength of one's character and devotion to God, post-modern persons see it as weakness, reserved only for people who are in danger of losing their faith. Quite the contrary. True humility is powerful because the attention is not focused on gratifying the self, but rather on fulfilling the needs of others. As John the Baptist put it, *"He (Jesus) must become greater; I must become less"* (John 3:30). Following Jesus is not about pointing to your accumulated possessions as proof of your faithfulness and blessings from God. Instead, true discipleship is based on following Jesus without becoming entangled in the cares and concerns of the world because the follower is secure in knowing that it is God who ultimately gets the credit for any and all life-transformational work. In other words, discipleship looks at every situation as a daily opportunity to serve rather than be served.

Likewise, taking up one's cross and following Jesus implies laying down your life for others. This is a very difficult thing to do. Thomas a' Kempis, a fifteenth century German-Dutch mystic wrote:

Jesus has always many who love His heavenly kingdom, but few who bear His cross. He has many who desire consolation, but few who care for trial. He finds many to share His table, but few to take part in His fasting. All desire to be happy with Him; few wish to suffer anything for Him. Many follow Him to the breaking of bread, but few to the drinking of the chalice of His passion. Many revere His miracles; few approach the shame of the Cross. Many love Him as long as they encounter no hardship; many praise and bless Him as long as they receive some comfort from Him. But if Jesus hides Himself and leaves them for a while, they fall either into complaints or into deep dejection. Those, on the contrary, who love Him for His own sake and not for any comfort of their own, bless Him in all trial and anguish of heart as well as in the bliss of consolation. Even if He should never give them consolation, yet they would continue to praise Him and wish always to give Him thanks. What power there is in pure love for Jesus — love that is free from all self-interest and self-love! (Knox, 1959).

It is interesting that in order to make this task of following Christ more appealing, some people go to great lengths to clean up the cross from its grotesque representation of first-century capital punishment. No longer are crosses reminders of blood-stained, rotting flesh planks of wood. Instead, they are often transformed into precious pieces of jewelry that people wear around their necks. Churches are often adorned with shiny replicas of the cross that have been polished in order to mask the revulsion and brutality of the suffering and death which Jesus embraced for us. This is hardly the original image that crosses portrayed in the first century.

I remember when Mel Gibson's movie *The Passion* came out in theaters. Everybody talked about how gut-wrenching it was to watch one bloody scene after another about the suffering and crucifixion of Jesus. Afterwards, many people remarked that it was too violent and graphic to show, even with an R-rating. However, I took a different approach. I believe it needed to be graphic and shock us to the point of nausea, because we needed to be reminded about the depth of Jesus' love for us, in order to rescue us from the depth of our depravity and sin. Furthermore, God's grace needed to be extreme because how often do human beings commit heinous crimes against one another? For example, how many times throughout history have people done unspeakable, horrendous things to each other? How many countless millions have been burned alive, buried alive and even mutilated? Perhaps we have become so conditioned by what we see each day that by cleaning up the cross, we want to shield ourselves on Sundays mornings from the cruelty humanity is capable of. Yet, it was for this reason Jesus embraced suffering, or as German Protestant theologian Jürgen Moltmann (1993) states, *"absorbed" suffering, in its extreme form in order to transform it once and for all so that we may be redeemed through his death and resurrection.*

Still, being redeemed by the blood of Jesus from our sins does not let us off the hook of responsibility to live out our faith on a daily basis. "Taking up our cross" also means taking up the suffering of the world in order to alleviate it in others. This is truly the definition of compassion, literally to "suffer with," and goes far beyond pity, but involves a will to act as well. For some people this involves direct, hands-on involvement working with local and national governments to alleviate poverty, oppression, slavery, etc. For others, providing prayer and financial support are some ways of being involved. Whatever the task, the focus must be on going back into the world to be the hands and feet of Christ.

Rev. Dr. Randy Nugent, now retired General Secretary of the General Board of Global Ministries, once told a story about his missionary work in a local hospital in an African village. Every week he noticed a young girl would arrive by herself at the clinic to receive medical care.

When he learned that the girl not only lived in another village miles and miles away, but also had access to a much closer hospital, he asked her why she chose to travel so far out of her way. Her response forever changed his life. Pointing to her palms she said, *"The people's hands are different here. They are kinder."* How we reach out to others is just as important as to whom we reach out. How will people know the love of Christ unless we first extend hands of grace and love? Some people might say it is a waste of time to reach out to those who do not want help. To this I reply, *"Is it not enough that we reach out in Christ name in the first place? You never know when the grace of God might take hold of a person's heart and forever change their soul."*

Exercise:

(1) Begin by sitting comfortably. Take several deep breaths. When you are ready, read Matthew 16:21-23, Mark 8:31-9:1 aloud. Silently meditate on these words. Make a note, which words resonate within your heart and soul. Perhaps you want to read aloud the quote from Thomas a' Kempis? What sentence or phrase gets your attention? Sit with these for several minutes.

(2) As you re-read the passage, interact with the story. Reflect on the story and imagine yourself as Peter as Jesus rebukes you for your lack of understanding. What do you hear/see/smell/feel as Jesus reproaches you?

.

(3) Re-read the passage. What is stirred in you as you hear Jesus describe discipleship as, "denying yourself, taking up the cross, and following him?" Ask God, "Where does this passage touch my life today?" What in my life keeps me from "denying myself?"

(4) Finally, ask yourself, "What is it that God wants me to do as a result of meditating on this passage?" What areas of my life do I need to live out my faith and devotion to God more fully?

Chapter 6

"Couldn't We Stay A Little Longer?"
Matthew 17:1-13, Mark 9:2-8, Luke 9:28-36

After six days Jesus took with him Peter, James and John the brother of James, and led them up a high mountain by themselves. There he was transfigured before them. His face shone like the sun, and his clothes became as white as the light. Just then there appeared before them Moses and Elijah, talking with Jesus. Peter said to Jesus, "Lord, it is good for us to be here. If you wish, I will put up three shelters—one for you, one for Moses and one for Elijah." While he was still speaking, a bright cloud enveloped them, and a voice from the cloud said, "This is my Son, whom I love; with him I am well pleased. Listen to him!" When the disciples heard this they fell face down to the ground, terrified. But

Jesus came and touched them. "Get up," he said, "Don't be afraid." When they looked up, they saw no one but Jesus.

Was there ever a time in your life when you felt the presence of God so close to you that you could reach out your hand and touch it? Perhaps it was a time when you felt God's peace so strongly that you just couldn't put it into words? Having grown up with a German background, I remember not too much was often said regarding "religious" experiences. My family's belief was that one's religion was a private matter between the person and God. Religion was not to be discussed. Ironically, my uncle Ed seemed to ignore this rule. In fact, during family picnics I would often hear about the time when he felt the power and peace of God. It was a time when his daughter, my cousin, was facing a life-threatening heart surgery. My uncle described it as a time when he had never been so worried and distraught in all of his life. He could not eat, sleep and found it difficult to concentrate on anything else. On the day of her surgery, he went to the chapel to pray by himself. As he was crying and pouring his heart to God, for the briefest second, he saw a flash of light go across his eyes. Immediately, he sensed a warm peace wash over him. He said he never felt anything like that before in his life. He knew in an instant that whether my cousin would live or die, she was in God's hands. I must have heard this story over 30 times. Everytime he told it, he would always get choked up, as if he were back in that chapel all over again.

Those times in our lives when we find ourselves in the midst of God's presence in a glorious and powerful way are what I would call "mountain-top" experiences! We never forget them, nor are we ever the same again. We cannot look at ourselves and others in the same way because our lives have been radically altered by the presence of God. Even if we wanted to go back to the former ways of thinking, we cannot because we have tasted something divine. In other words, God has stepped in and provided us a glimpse of heaven.

In this passage, Peter, James and John go up to a mountain with Jesus and he is transfigured before their eyes. As his countenance was a brilliant display of glory and majesty, a cloud enveloped them as they heard the voice of God say, *"This is my Son; listen to him!"* And what a sight it must have been for Peter to see Moses and Elijah! We might imagine Peter's face flushed with exhilaration. No wonder he wanted to stay up there! We would too! Personally, I do not believe it was by accident that Moses and Elijah were there on the mountain with Jesus, Peter, James and John. In fact, from a theological standpoint it could be argued that Jesus was seen in that moment as the greater fulfillment of the Law (Moses) and the Prophets (Elijah).

Nevertheless, I believe there is another lesson in this passage for us to learn regarding mountain-top experiences. Moses and Elijah were no strangers to experiencing the glory of God. In fact, both men had their share of mountain-top experiences. Moses had spent 40 days and nights in the presence of God as he received the commandments:

Moses said to the LORD, "You have been telling me, 'Lead these people,' but you have not let me know whom you will send with me. You have said, 'I know you by name and you have found favor with me.' If you are pleased with me, teach me your ways so I may know you and continue to find favor with you. Remember that this nation is your people." The LORD replied, "My Presence will go with you, and I will give you rest."

Then Moses said to him, "If your Presence does not go with us, do not send us up from here. How will anyone know that you are pleased with me and with your people unless you go with us? What else will distinguish me and your people from all the other people on the face of the earth?" And the LORD said to Moses, "I will do the very thing you have asked, because I am pleased with you and I know you by name." Then Moses said, "Now show me your glory."

And the LORD said, "I will cause all my good-
ness to pass in front of you, and I will proclaim my
name, the LORD, in your presence. I will have mercy
on whom I will have mercy, and I will have compas-
sion on whom I will have compassion. But," he said,
"you cannot see my face, for no one may see me and
live." Then the LORD said, "There is a place near
me where you may stand on a rock. When my glory
passes by, I will put you in a cleft in the rock and
cover you with my hand until I have passed by. Then
I will remove my hand and you will see my back; but
my face must not be seen."

When Moses came down from Mount Sinai with
the two tablets of the Testimony in his hands, he
was not aware that his face was radiant because
he had spoken with the LORD. When Aaron and
all the Israelites saw Moses, his face was radiant,
and they were afraid to come near him. But Moses
called to them; so Aaron and all the leaders of the
community came back to him, and he spoke to them.
Afterward all the Israelites came near him, and he
gave them all the commands the LORD had given
him on Mount Sinai.

When Moses finished speaking to them, he put
a veil over his face. But whenever he entered the
LORD's presence to speak with him, he removed the

veil until he came out. And when he came out and told the Israelites what he had been commanded, they saw that his face was radiant. Then Moses would put the veil back over his face until he went in to speak with the LORD. (Exodus 33:12-23, 29-35).

Elijah's mountaintop experience came when he battled the priests of Baal on top of Mount Carmel:

So Obadiah went to meet Ahab and told him, and Ahab went to meet Elijah. When he saw Elijah, he said to him, "Is that you, you troubler of Israel?" "I have not made trouble for Israel," Elijah replied. "But you and your father's family have. You have abandoned the LORD's commands and have followed the Baals. Now summon the people from all over Israel to meet me on Mount Carmel. And bring the four hundred and fifty prophets of Baal and the four hundred prophets of Asherah, who eat at Jezebel's table."

So Ahab sent word throughout all Israel and assembled the prophets on Mount Carmel. Elijah went before the people and said, "How long will you waver between two opinions? If the LORD is God, follow him; but if Baal is God, follow him." But the people said nothing.

Then Elijah said to them, "I am the only one of the LORD's prophets left, but Baal has four hundred and fifty prophets. Get two bulls for us. Let them choose one for themselves, and let them cut it into pieces and put it on the wood but not set fire to it. I will prepare the other bull and put it on the wood but not set fire to it. Then you call on the name of your god, and I will call on the name of the LORD. The god who answers by fire—he is God." Then all the people said, "What you say is good."

Elijah said to the prophets of Baal, "Choose one of the bulls and prepare it first, since there are so many of you. Call on the name of your god, but do not light the fire." So they took the bull given them and prepared it. Then they called on the name of Baal from morning till noon. "O Baal, answer us!" they shouted. But there was no response; no one answered. And they danced around the altar they had made.

At noon Elijah began to taunt them. "Shout louder!" he said. "Surely he is a god! Perhaps he is deep in thought, or busy, or traveling. Maybe he is sleeping and must be awakened." So they shouted louder and slashed themselves with swords and spears, as was their custom, until their blood flowed. Midday passed, and they continued their frantic prophesying until the time for the evening sacrifice.

But there was no response, no one answered, no one paid attention.

Then Elijah said to all the people, "Come here to me." They came to him, and he repaired the altar of the LORD, which was in ruins. Elijah took twelve stones, one for each of the tribes descended from Jacob, to whom the word of the LORD had come, saying, "Your name shall be Israel." With the stones he built an altar in the name of the LORD, and he dug a trench around it large enough to hold two seahs of seed. He arranged the wood, cut the bull into pieces and laid it on the wood. Then he said to them, "Fill four large jars with water and pour it on the offering and on the wood." "Do it again," he said, and they did it again. "Do it a third time," he ordered, and they did it the third time. The water ran down around the altar and even filled the trench.

At the time of sacrifice, the prophet Elijah stepped forward and prayed: "O LORD, God of Abraham, Isaac and Israel, let it be known today that you are God in Israel and that I am your servant and have done all these things at your command. Answer me, O LORD, answer me, so these people will know that you, O LORD, are God, and that you are turning their hearts back again." Then the fire of the LORD fell and burned up the sacrifice, the wood, the stones and the soil, and also licked up the water in the trench. When all the people saw this, they fell prostrate and cried, "The LORD -he is God! The LORD -he is God!" (1 Kings 18:17-18:39, NIV)

Pretty impressive, right? Yet despite having witnessed God's glory and majesty first-hand, these mountain-top experiences of Moses and Elijah are only half of the story. The other half involves coming down from the mountain and being faced with unpleasant realities. When Moses came down from mountain the first time, he saw the Israelites dancing and worshipping the golden calf they made. Immediately filled with shock and disbelief, he threw down the stone tablets upon which the law of God was written, smashing them into pieces (Exodus 32:15-20). Likewise, when Elijah came down from his mountain-top experience, he fled for his life because of the price Jezebel put on his head for killing her false prophets and priests (1 Kings 19:1-3).

Although we may have not been entrusted with delivering God's law or defeating the prophets of Baal, sooner or later we realize we must come down from the mountain and go through our own valleys of contention, struggle and trouble. However, we must never forget those times when we have tasted the power, majesty and glory of God. Perhaps we experience a strong presence of the Lord through uplifting praise and worship. Other times our hearts may be quickened by an answer to a long-awaited prayer. There may even be times when we are simply encouraged in our spirits when others have been blessed by God. Either way, these blessings manifest God's glory which give us hope in times of despair and an inner strength to go through difficult times.

A common feature of the mountain-top experience is often what happens after we come down from the mountain and face everyday life. We are hit with reality of everyday demands, schedules and problems. For example, I remember one Sunday service that was particularly powerful. It was Confirmation Sunday and we had eight students who were ready to declare their faith publicly and join the local church. One of the rituals I do in this service is have the teens take communion, then laying my hands on them I pronounce a blessing over them as they profess their faith. There was not a single dry eye in the congregation as we all sensed the peace of God wash over us. At one point, there was complete silence, because nobody wanted to say or do anything; the presence of God was so strong. I was grateful and humbled for the way the Holy Spirit touched everyone there. Driving home from the service I remember thanking God for such a blessing and the gift of His presence. When I arrived home, I received a phone call that a parishoner's mother was dying in the hospital. She asked me to come because the family needed me to help them. When I arrived at the hospital, the family was indeed in turmoil. There was a lot of confusion about what to do and when to do it. Some extended family members could not be reached and were unaware their loved-one was dying. There was a strong element of chaos and confusion indeed. Still, being reminded of God's grace and peace earlier in the day, I was able to offer a reassuring presence to the family. Funny how quickly our lives may go from one extreme to another; yet God remains constant.

This sounds a lot like what Peter experienced after his mountain-top experience. Matthew's gospel tells us that when the disciples came down from the mountain, they were immediately met by a boy with a demon (Matthew 17:14-16). Not only did the boy suffer from seizures, but the demon would also make him fall into fire and water. Talk about chaos! Nonetheless, the boy was healed by Jesus. I imagine Peter's head must have felt as if it was on a roller coaster of emotions, wondering when the ride would come to a stop! Perhaps Peter's story reminds us not to take for granted those tangible moments when we are aware of God's presence in our lives. Instead of interpreting these mountain-top experiences as short-lived and quickly evaporating, perhaps we would be able to recognize more of God's presence in our lives, if we first make ourselves available to God everyday. Taking time each day to sit quietly and meditate on scripture sensitizes us to the still, small stirring of the Holy Spirit in our hearts. Some people develop this sensitivity to God's presence by engaging in contemplative prayer.

Throughout history, Christians such as Teresa of Avila, John of the Cross, and Francis of Assisi, Thomas Merton and many others, devoted their lives to this way of praying. These were people who experienced God in life-changing ways because they quieted their minds and invited God into the walls of their souls. They were willing to embrace the shadow parts of themselves, understanding them not as defects, but as opportunities for spiritual growth. As Thomas Merton puts it:

"Contemplative prayer has to be always very simple, confined to the simplest of acts and using no words or thoughts. This prayer of the heart introduces us into deep interior silence so that we learn to experience its power. We seek the deepest ground of our identity with God - a direct experiential grasp just like St. Augustine sought when he prayed, 'May I know you, may I know myself.'" (*Contemplative Prayer*, 1971)

Exercise:

(1) Begin by sitting comfortably. Take several deep breaths. When you are ready, read Matthew 17:1-13, Mark 9:2-8, or Luke 9:28-34 aloud. Silently meditate on these words. Make a note, which words resonate within your heart and soul. What sentence or phrase gets your atten-

tion? Sit with these for several minutes. Perhaps you may choose to reflect on the complete prayer of St. Augustine quoted in this chapter. If so, what is the interplay between knowing God and knowing yourself? How does this awareness affect your relationships with your family, friends, co-workers, enemies?

(2) As you re-read the passage, interact with the story. Imagine yourself climbing this mountain with Jesus. "How far will Jesus climb?" "What is Jesus' purpose?" Stand on this mountain and imagine what you can see from a distance? What do you see, hear and smell as Jesus is transfigured before you? What do you sense when the cloud envelopes you and you hear God's voice, *"This is my Son, whom I love; with him I am well pleased. Listen to him!"*

(3) Re-read the passage. Ask God, "Where does this passage touch my life today?" "What have been my mountain-top experiences where I clearly sensed your presence?" "How have they changed me and my perspectives on life?" "How have these experiences equipped me for dealing with life-situations after you have come down from the mountain?"

(4) Finally, ask yourself, "What it is that God wants me to do now as a result of meditating on this passage?" "What shadow areas of my life do I need to embrace and see as opportunities for spiritual growth and maturity?"

The Confessions of St. Augustine, Bishop of Hippo
Translated by Henry Chadwick (1998)
Book X, Chapter 1

LET me know Thee, O Thou who knowest me;
let me know Thee, as I am known.
O Thou strength of my soul, enter into it,
and prepare it for Thyself,
that Thou mayest have and hold it without
"spot or wrinkle."
This is my hope, "therefore have I spoken";
and in this hope do I rejoice, when I rejoice soberly.
Other things of this life ought the less to be sorrowed for,
the more they are sorrowed for;
and ought the more to be sorrowed for,
the less men do sorrow for them.
For behold, "Thou desirest truth,"
seeing that he who does it "cometh to the light."
This wish I to do in confession in my heart before Thee,
and in my writing before many witnesses.

Chapter 7

"The Lesson at the Bottom of a Cracker-Jack Box"
Matthew 17:24-27

*A*fter *Jesus and his disciples arrived at Capernaum, the collectors of the two-drachma tax came to Peter and asked, "Doesn't your teacher pay the temple tax?" "Yes, he does," he replied. When Peter came into the house, Jesus was the first to speak. "What do you think, Simon?" he asked, "From whom do the kings of the earth collect duty and taxes—from their own sons, or from others?" "From others," Peter answered. "Then the sons are exempt," Jesus said to him. "But that we may not offend them, go to the lake and thrown out your line. Take the first fish you catch; open its mouth and you will find a four-drachma coin. Take it and give it to them for your tax and mine."*

Be honest. What's the best part about eating a box of Cracker Jacks? Of course! Getting the prize at the bottom of the box. Oh, I'll admit that I enjoyed eating the toffee-drenched popcorn and nuts too. But I think everyone tried to stick his/her hand down in the box to feel for that prize: A match-box size comic book, water tattoo, plastic whistles, etc. These prizes weren't anything of value, except to the one who bought the box in the first place. I wonder if Peter had this same excitement in anticipating what Jesus had in mind when he told him to get a fish out of the lake. Perhaps he was still wondering what Jesus was up to? Why couldn't Jesus come right out and say what he meant? Why does there always have to be an object-lesson involved, and it usually involved fish on some level? You know, for a carpenter, Jesus really liked to tell Peter how to fish. Think about it. All of the stories we have of Peter fishing, the only time a catch is noted was when Jesus instructs him when, where and how to fish. You think that after a while Peter would catch on. But then again, we probably wouldn't either.

On one level we could read this passage to understand how God meets our needs. In the story Jesus and Peter needed to pay their taxes, but where would they get the money? I know! Peter you just go down to the lake, cast your line and the first fish you catch will contain enough money for our temple-tax to be paid. Simple? Yes, but a little too simple. There's much more to the story than finding money when you need it. The answer is to be found in Jesus' analogy of rulers and the tribute owed to them. Interestingly, this conversation takes place regarding the temple, the physical place where worship and sacrifices are offered. Since the kings of the earth only collect taxes from those they govern and not their own children, it stands to reason: Since Jesus is God's Son, and the temple is his Father's house, he then is exempt from paying the temple tax. Likewise, since the disciples are also part of the family of God, they too are exempt. What Jesus was saying was that because his death on the cross will be the ultimate sacrifice for sin, there will no longer be a need for a temple where animal sacrifices were offered. The place where people could embrace the future promise of redemption and forgiveness of sins now would see the fulfillment in Jesus' sacrificial death on the cross. As a result, the "sons and daughters" of God would be set free from sin's obligation by Jesus' paying the price for all sins:

> *When Christ came as high priest of the good things that are already here, he went through the greater and more perfect tabernacle that is not man-made, that is to say, not a part of this creation. He did not enter by means of the blood of goats and calves; but he entered the Most Holy Place once for all by his own blood, having obtained eternal redemption. The blood of goats and bulls and the ashes of a heifer*

sprinkled on those who are ceremonially unclean sanctify them so that they are outwardly clean. How much more, then, will the blood of Christ, who through the eternal Spirit offered himself unblemished to God, cleanse our consciences from acts that lead to death, so that we may serve the living God! For this reason Christ is the mediator of a new covenant, that those who are called may receive the promised eternal inheritance—now that he has died as a ransom to set them free from the sins committed under the first covenant (Hebrews 9:11-15).

Likewise,

The law is only a shadow of the good things that are coming—not the realities themselves. For this reason it can never, by the same sacrifices repeated endlessly year after year, make perfect those who draw near to worship. If it could, would they not have stopped being offered? For the worshipers would have been cleansed once for all, and would no longer have felt guilty for their sins. But those sacrifices are an annual reminder of sins, because it is impossible for the blood of bulls and goats to take away sins.

Therefore, when Christ came into the world, he said: "Sacrifice and offering you did not desire, but a body you prepared for me; with burnt offerings and sin offerings you were not pleased. Then I said, 'Here I am—it is written about me in the scroll—I have come to do your will, O God.' First he said, "Sacrifices and offerings, burnt offerings and sin offerings you did not desire, nor were you pleased with them" (although the law required them to be made). Then he said, "Here I am, I have come to do your will." He sets aside the first to establish the second. And by that will, we have been made holy through the sacrifice of the body of Jesus Christ once for all (Hebrews 10:1-10).

Many people wrestle with guilt, guilt over things they might have said in anger or haste; guilt over what they have done or didn't do. In my opinion, working with someone wrestling with guilt is easier than working with someone wrestling with shame. What's the difference? First of all, unlike guilt, shame involves a person's internalizing negative feelings of self-worth. At the extreme, shame can become very toxic as the person is convinced he or she is incapable of loving and being loved. Self-talk such as, "I am worthless, no good, evil, wicked, etc.," play over and over again in one's mind. Also, personal attempts of accomplishing anything are often met with self-sabotaging behavior, which only rein-forces this negative belief about oneself. Remember Peter's first encounter with Jesus in Luke 5:1-11? *"Away from me, Lord, for I am a sinner!"* This is shame talking. Peter believed he was nothing more than this. Christ saw differently, and called him to discover far more than he might imagined.

On the other hand, guilt focuses on past action. With the benefit of hindsight, guilt involves regret over something we have said or done (committed), or what we did not say or do (omitted). What makes guilt so immobilizing for many people is that they simple cannot believe Christ's sacrificial death and resurrection cleanses them not only from sin, but also the guilt that comes from having wronged others. In other words, people sometimes have a harder time forgiving themselves. As "Tom," a 40 year old man put it to me: *"I know God has forgiven me, but I cannot seem to let go of feeling guilty. Every time I start to feel good about helping others, I am reminded of past mistakes."* As we probed this powerful statement some more, Tom discovered that his drive for perfectionism when he was young kept him from forgiving himself for anything less than being "perfect." The turning point came for Tom when I suggested he have a mock funeral for his imperfections. First, he was to make a list of everything in his past that he felt guilty about. If he wronged another person, then he was to go and ask forgiveness. If there were times when he was wronged, then he was to seek out the person who wronged him and try to make amends. In both incidences, if forgiveness was not offered or accepted by the other person(s), then he would write about this experience, noting how the attempt was made. Finally, after his list was complete, he was then to dig a hole in his backyard and bury the list and mark it with a cross with the date written on it. Then, every time those thoughts and feelings of guilt would emerge, he would simply have to look at the cross in his yard, and remind himself that those sins he committed have been "buried with Christ" (Colossians 2:12).

Another good image that works with people wrestling with guilt is to describe their "faults" in terms of physical weight. For some people, guilt feels as if they're carrying around an extra 25-50 lbs! One might suggest why would a person carry around so much additional weight when all they have to do is simply put it down? This is easier said than done, especially when it comes to the weight of emotions. To drive this image home, I suggest people carry a 10-15lb. weight with them everywhere they go for a week. They are not allowed to hide the weight in a bookbag, briefcase, or purse. Instead, they are to literally carry this weight to the grocery store, the bathroom, a restaurant, to work and/or school, etc. After a day, if it takes that long, people realize the futility of carrying around this physical burden, and they begin to make changes in their lives to alleviate the emotional guilt. Interestingly, the life-changing transformation comes when people are astonished to find just how much their "guilt" has weighed them down from enjoying life. But then again, it's amazing what we get used to over time, isn't it?

Exercise:

(1) Begin by sitting comfortably. Take several deep breaths. When you are ready, read Matthew 17:24-27 aloud. Silently meditate on these words. Make a note, which words resonate within your heart and soul. What sentence or phrase gets your attention? Sit with these for several minutes.

(2) As you re-read the passage, interact with the story. Reflect on the story and imagine yourself within the temple grounds. Imagine the various sights, sounds and smell of activity within the temple. Imagine yourself sitting with Jesus in the temple. What other images come up for you?

(3) Re-read the passage. Ask God, "Where does this passage touch my life today? Where do I need to expand my understanding of the significance of Christ's sacrificial death for my sins? What are some things I have been doing that now take on new meaning in the light of Christ? How has this changed me and my perspectives on life? Where in my life do I still wrestle with guilt over

having said or done things that wronged others? How much am I 'weighed down' by feelings of guilt?"

(4) Finally, ask yourself, "What it is that God wants me to do now as a result of meditating on this passage?" If you have chosen the task of literally carrying around a ten pound weight as a symbol of your burdens, ask yourself: "What in my life is weighing me down? What would I like to get rid of? What would I like to take hold of more? What are shadow areas of my life that I need to embrace and see as opportunities for spiritual growth and maturity? How can I help unburden others from what weighs them down, or their feelings of guilt?"

Chapter 8

"Limitless Forgiveness"
Matthew 18:15-22

" *If your brother sins against you, go and show him his fault, just between the two of you. If he listens to you, you have won your brother over. But if he will not listen, take one or two others along, so that every matter may be established by the testimony of two or three witnesses. If he refuses to listen to them, tell it to the church; and if he refuses to listen to the church, treat him as you would a pagan or a tax collector. I tell you the truth, whatever you bind on earth is bound in heaven, and whatever you loose on earth will be loosed in heaven. Again, I tell you that if two of you agree on anything you ask for, it will be done for you by my Father in heaven. For where two or three are gathered in my name, there I am with them. Then Peter came up to Jesus and asked, "Lord, how many times shall I forgive my brother when he*

sins against me? Up to seven times?" Jesus answered, "I tell you, not seven times, but seventy times seven."

I love going to flea markets. It seems as though you can find anything you're looking for at them. Of course, the best time to go is first thing in the morning, because that's when you can get a hot sausage sandwich, fries and coffee to start your day. I know, it's not the breakfast of champions, but it does warm you up on a brisk morning! At one such flea market, I saw a fine display of *welcome mats* all in a variety of shapes and sizes. Some were made out of carpet, some consisted of astroturf and rubber, and there were some made out of wood. As I stood there admiring the intricate details of these mats, I did not buy one because I couldn't see myself wiping my muddy shoes, and eventually marring the beautiful designs.

There was a time when I was visiting a family from Bosnia for whom our church had sponsored their relocation to the United States. They spoke very little English and lived in a modest apartment, but their hospitality was overwhelming. One of the family traditions they enjoyed was inviting people over for dinners, which were nothing short of magnificent! The food was unbelievable! Bread, rice, dried fruit, cheese, fresh vegetables, some roasted meat, and of course, extra strong coffee that would start to dissolve my fillings. The first time I was invited to one of these dinners,

I realized the mother spoke no English and I communicated mainly through her son and oldest daughter. When they opened the door I was immediately invited inside. However, before doing so, I quickly reached down to take off my shoes and leave them outside, so as not to offend them. When I straightened up, I saw the mother smiling at me and nodding in approval of my respect for their home and hospitality. From that moment on, I was treated as a long-lost family member.

I am convinced that wiping our shoes on a mat, or taking off our shoes altogether before enter the home of another, is a standard cultural practice. However, despite the beautiful embroidered "Welcome" sign we see staring up at us, that's essentially what a mat is for, to wipe our shoes. People are not. Think about a doormat. It's flat and lifeless. It just lies there and may be stepped on several times a day from people going in or out of a house or office building. Now imagine everywhere you walk in any given day. Experts tell us that we take, on the average, up to 10,000 steps (roughly five miles) each day. To test this theory, we can count our steps by wearing a device called a *pedometer*, or we can just pay attention to where we walk each day. We take walks with friends, walk the dog, use stairs instead of an elevator, walk around a store to make a purchase or down the hall to see a co-worker. No wonder the first thing most people at the end of the day is to take off their shoes! Our feet have been everywhere! We come in contact with a lot of dirt, grime, water, dust, mud, feces particles, etc. We also may come in contact with a lot of hurt. In any given day, we may experience the pain of rejection, betrayal, loss, etc. That kind of "soil" does not come off so easily as when we wipe our shoes. In fact, perhaps without ever realizing it, we simply bring that pain with us as we step over the threshhold of our homes.

Whenever the subject of forgiveness comes up in discussion groups or individual counseling, I'm amazed just how often people associate it with the image of a doormat. It's not that people don't understand what forgiveness is all about, but instead most of their resistance to forgive others comes from an unwillingness to let go of an offense. For some, they want to make sure that the one who has offended them suffers emotionally and/or physically as much as they have. Forgiveness, on the other hand, transforms the offense, and says, *"I'm not here for you to wipe your feet on, but if you want to come inside, you must first take off your shoes."*

Many people feel like doormats. They believe they are here on earth to do nothing more than absorb the dirt and grime that has been wiped on them by others. When Jesus told Peter that he had to forgive 70 times 7, this was not a literal number of 490. Jesus was not telling Peter, nor us, to literally keep track of the number of times we have forgiven. If we do this, we will be tempted to show off about it, or hold it out there like a cheap virtue for everyone to gasp at and envy. No, what Jesus is saying is that we should be ready to forgive, as much as it is needed. Do everything in your power to reconcile and be reconciled. If this is not possible, then by taking two or three other people with us demonstrates our willingness to peacefully resolve the matter.

Of course, when we are hurt we may not feel like forgiving, but we need to remember that just like grief, forgiveness is a process. We may not have the strength one day to forgive an entire offense, but can we forgive a little bit? Can we work toward total forgiveness by taking smaller steps of acknowledging our pain, talking with the person who hurt us, or even asking ourselves why is it so difficult for us to let go of our unforgiveness? Is it a power issue? Do we think that if we forgive, then we have surrendered our trump card? If we forgive, do we then have nothing left to pull out that would empower us to hold the offense over another's head. Ironically, forgiveness does empower us. Forgiveness trumps evil. Forgiveness disarms rage. Forgiveness turns aside vengeance. Forgiveness starts the healing process.

Several years ago I saw the off-Broadway play, *The Laramie Project* in Philadelphia. The story depicted the life of Matthew Sheppard, who was found tied to a fence, beaten, and died five days later of wounds to his face and head. Despite the rampant political and religious themes that ran through the story, I found myself focusing on the boy who found Matthew's body that day. All throughout the play, this boy struggled with the reason why *he* was the first one to find Matthew. According to him, he was simply riding his bike that day on a road he had never been on before, when he came upon Matthew's body. Throughout the play his character would come in and out of scenes trying to reconcile how Matthew died, the media's attention and the town's diverse emotional reactions and opinions. At the closing scene, this boy is the only character left on stage. He states that he has finally realized why it was he who found Matthew that day: To start the healing. Whether forgiving ourselves or another, being willing to forgive indeed begins the healing process. Marianne Williamson (*The Power of Forgiveness*, 2007) states that *"we live in a time when there is a great deal of evil around us. As a result, we must hold those who deal in evil responsible for their actions. Nevertheless, we must also stand for the possibility of human redemption that turns even the hardest hearts. Forgiveness is not about forgetting. Instead, forgiveness is being able to let go of the pain in the memory."*

Exercise:

(1) Begin by sitting comfortably. Take several deep breaths. When you are ready, read Matthew 18:15-22 aloud. Silently meditate on these words. Make a note, which words resonate within your heart and soul. What sentence

or phrase gets your attention? Sit with these for several minutes. Perhaps you may choose to read and reflect on the quote by Archbishop Desmond Tutu in *No Future Without Forgiveness*. If so, ask yourself, "How does the 'action' of forgiveness impact me and my relationships with God and others?"

(2) As you re-read the passage, interact with the story. Reflect on the story and imagine your reaction to Jesus' words about forgiveness. Remember those times when you have offended others and/or been offended. What feelings do you notice in yourself? Jealousy, anger, embarrassment, rage, shame, guilt, etc.?

(3) Re-read the passage. Ask God, "Where does this passage touch my life today? Where in my life do I still wrestle with unforgiveness? What are the reasons why you hang on to your unwillingness to forgive others? Where does the *pain in the memory* still linger for you? How do you see your life differently if you would forgive?"

(4) Finally, ask yourself, "What it is that God wants me to do now as a result of meditating on this passage? What shadow areas of my life do I need to embrace and see as opportunities to redeem others from their unwillingness to forgive?"

No Future Without Forgiveness
Archbishop Desmond Tutu (2000)

"Forgiveness and reconciliation are not cheap, they are costly. Forgiveness does not condone or minimize the awfulness of an atrocity or wrong. It is to recognize its ghastliness but to choose to acknowledge the essential humanity of the perpetrator and to give that perpetrator the possibility of making a new beginning. Forgiveness is an act of much hope and not despair. It is to hope in the essential goodness of people and to have faith in their potential to change. It is to bet on that possibility. Forgiveness, is not opposed to justice, especially if it is not punitive justice, but restorative justice, justice that does not seek primary to punish the perpetrator, to hit out, but looks to heal a breach, to restore social equilibrium that the atrocity or misdeed has disturbed. Ultimately there is no future without forgiveness."

Chapter 9

The Therapeutic Bind
John 6:53-69

*J*esus said to them, *"I tell you the truth, unless you eat the flesh of the Son of Man and drink his blood, you have no life in you. Whoever eats my flesh and drinks my blood has eternal life, and I will raise him up at the last day. For my flesh is real food and my blood is real drink. Whoever eats my flesh and drinks my blood remains in me and I in him. Just as the living Father has sent me and I live because of the Father, so the one who feeds on me will live because of me. This is the bread that came down from heaven. Your forefathers ate manna and died, but he who feeds on this bread will live forever."* He said this while teaching in the synagogue in Capernaum. On hearing it, many of his disciples said, *"This is a hard teaching. Who can accept it?*

Aware that his disciples were grumbling about this, Jesus said to them, "Does this offend you? What if you see the Son of Man ascend to where he was before! The Spirit gives life; the flesh counts for nothing. The words I have spoken to you are spirit and they are life. Yet, there are some of you who do not believe." For Jesus had known from the beginning which of them did not believe and who would betray him. He went on to say, This is why I told you that no one can come to me unless the Father enables him." From this time many of his disciples turned back and no longer followed him. "You do not want to leave too, do you?" Jesus asked the Twelve. Simon Peter answered him, "Lord, to whom shall we go? You have the words of eternal life. We believe you are the Holy One of God."

I often say that God doesn't play fair. When I first felt God stirring my heart to enter ministry, little did I realize how persistent God is. The more I pushed away the desires of God, the stronger they returned, until I yield to them. I was in my early twenties and developed a strong desire to lead others in a greater understanding of God's promises contained in Scripture. The only problem was that I was a nervous wreck. Every time I stood up to speak, I shook, literally. Fortunately for me, I was just as stubborn as I was nervous. I determined that I in order to overcome my anxiety, I would stand up to it and face it head-on! Still, week after week, I tortured myself by struggling through lesson after painful lesson loaded with mispronounced words, fumbling papers, and endless trivial details. Yet one thing continued to emerge: the deep desire to see people changed by God's grace. Little did I realize in whom God was bringing about the change. For example, one Sunday morning was particularly transforming for me. Before the lesson I gave God an ultimatum: *"Ok, I tried to tackle this problem myself, so either cure me of my nervousness or choose someone else more qualified!"* Ever notice how often God answers those prayers we speak in haste, while other prayers seem to go unanswered? Anyway, that morning I typically struggled through the lesson. Nervously, I tried to keep my notes from falling out of my Bible as I taught on God's mercy from my own life experiences. By the time the lesson was over, my shirt was soaked, papers were stuffed haphazardly in my Bible, and I was finished; f inished with God asking me to do something I didn't enjoy; finished with puzzling looks on people's faces staring back at me as I quickly jumped from example to example in my lessons. I was finished. Period. Oh, I justified my decision to God by stating that I gave it my best shot, stepped out in faith and trusted that if it was meant to be, God would hold up the other end of the bargain.

As I gathered my things and headed for my car, I was surprised to hear a man's voice calling for me to wait. I turned around and saw a man whom I had known casually.

He had a gentle smile on his face and a note of sincerity in his voice. He said he wanted to catch me before I left and thank me for explaining that passage of Scripture so well. He had never quite understood the meaning until that morning and as a result, felt a tremendous sense of peace in his heart. I thanked him for his kind words, shook his hand and watched him walk away beaming from ear to ear. I stood there for a moment and realized what had just happened. I looked up to heaven as if I were directly looking into the eyes of God and said, *"You're not going to let me out of this, are you?"* No, God was not going to let me out of this call. Instead, God wanted me to learn a very valuable lesson: Effective ministry has more to do with God's faithfulness, than my abilities. In other words, it wasn't about me, but God working in and through me. I didn't need to worry about whether or not people would sense anxiety in me, as long as *they* experienced the peace of God. I didn't need to worry about how strong my voice would be, as long as people heard God's voice. Still, I needed to fulfill my end of the call by remaining faithful in my studies, prayer-life, and growing in my awareness of the Holy Spirit's leading.

Needless to say over the years, I have developed a deep appreciation for Peter's words in John 6:69, *"Lord, to whom shall we go? You have the words of eternal life."* I don't believe there ever was a Christian who has walked with God that has not been tempted at some point to walk away. After all, we face tremendous and overwhelming circumstances. At times life can be filled with disappointment, confusion, loss, hate, despair, disillusionment, frailty, temptation, physical and mental diagnosis, sadness, misery, pain, brokenness, etc. On the other hand, our lives are also filled with joy, peace, contentment, love, fulfillment, grace, happiness, celebrations, etc. The spiritual journey God calls us to walk is never unveiled all at once. Instead, we often catch a glimpse of it unfolding the more we yield our lives. If God were to unroll His plan for us all at once, we probably would run away, vowing that the task is too daunting and dangerous, leaving us feeling ill-equipped to undertake the challenges.

In explaining "God's plan for us" with children and youth, I often use a tangible object lesson. I take a piece of paper and repeatedly fold it until I have a small square. With each fold, I write a word on the space, which becomes hidden the moment I make another fold. When I'm finished I say, *"This folded up piece of paper is God's will for our lives. We can't see the end, i.e., what's written on the last fold, unless we begin by yielding ourselves by faith in God to reveal another section of God's plan for our lives. What we find is that as God's plan for our lives unfolds before us, God's grace enables us to take the next step by faith."* The looks on the youth's (and adults') faces are priceless! They quickly are able to make the connection between this lesson and their lives. I have also noticed that not only is the look of fear gone in the faces of the youth and adults, but also they feel empowered. As one youth shared with me later, *"God's plan for me isn't so frightening after all, because I know that God is with me!"* Bingo!

Funny how often we tend to complicate matters of faith. For some, human logic doesn't jive with God's wisdom. Can't you hear the initial exasperation in Peter's voice in this passage? *"What? Did I just hear you correctly, Jesus? Did you say that if we, your disciples, are offended by your words, you would allow us to walk away from you?"* Yes Peter, you heard correctly. Unbelievable as it sounded. After all that they have been through, given up and given over for Jesus, he was giving his disciples the freedom to walk away. Talk about putting Peter in a therapeutic bind! That's that little phenomena in a counseling situation that occurs when you are confronted with a life-changing decision. The choice is so obviously clear: You either embrace a new-found perspective and direction for your life, or remain in your current, often times, miserable situation. For those who listened to Jesus' words that day, he confronted them to make that kind of decision. He wanted them to go to the next level, as it were, in their spiritual understanding, transformation and commitment. Jesus' words of "eating his flesh and drinking his blood" were never meant to be taken literally. Eating blood was forbidden because it contained the life of any given creature, and thus was sacred to God (Genesis 9:4,

Leviticus 17:15). Instead, using the analogy of consuming food, that becomes life-giving by partaking of Jesus' death and resurrection via Holy Communion, and thus provides the ultimate life-giving nourishment for eternity. This understanding was something the crowd did not grasp, let alone want to explore further. Eventually, they turned away and followed Jesus no more (verse 66). Without missing a beat, Jesus offered the same exit strategy to his disciples. *"You do not want to leave too, do you?"* Simon Peter answered him, *"Lord, to whom shall we go? You have the words of eternal life. We believe you are the Holy One of God."* Whew! Thank you, Peter. Thank you that you got the underlying message and made the decision to go deeper in your relationship with Christ. Chalk one up for the therapeutic bind!

Unfortunately, when confronted with the therapeutic bind, some people freeze, unable to make a decision. Not knowing what that deeper commitment looks like, many people are immobilized by fear. Perhaps their pain, abuse, and sorrow have been with them for so long that any kind of healing is alarming. As one woman whom I was counseling put it to me: *"If you take away my pain, I have nothing else to hold on to."* You see, her whole identity was wrapped up in a lifetime of pain she had grown accustomed to. Was she suffering and lonely? Yes. Yet in her mind, she could not imagine her life apart from that misery. The same is true in our relationship with Christ. Some people will only go so far with Jesus. They typically justify their reasons why they have chosen to remain in their current parched state of spiritual alienation. They might say, *"Jesus let me down. Jesus disappointed me. Jesus didn't live up to my expectations. My life wasn't supposed to turn out this way!"* No matter how you slice it, it typically comes down to an unwillingness to conform to Christ. Instead, most people would rather have God conform to their expectations and lifestyles, than surrender themselves to God's will.

When you think about it, to be given the freedom to walk away from God is a scary thing. But then again, that's the nature of love. Love does not coerce, remember? It does not demand, it does not insist. It simply offers unconditional acceptance (1 Corinthians 13). Quite frankly, this is a hard concept to grasp especially since we live in a world that places so many conditions on love. Kelly was this way. Kelly was a 15-year-old girl I counseled for severe depression. By all outward appearances she looked like a normal teenager. She was very active in school: student council president, cheerleader, school dance committee chair, and active in her church youth group. Beneath the surface, Kelly's home-life was in turmoil. Kelly's parents were divorced and like most middle-born children, she was trying to hold things together in hopes that her parents would reunite. It never happened. For 10 years she told herself that if she would be a model student and a good daughter, then her parents would reconcile. I saw Kelly a month after she had learned that her father was going to marry another woman he had been dating for over a year. Inspite of her hopes to reunite her family, she had to let go and work on accepting how she and her family were changing.

One day I asked Kelly about her definition of love and she replied in a matter-of-fact tone of voice, *"I don't."* *"Don't what?"* I asked. *"I don't love. Because when you love, you're vulnerable."* Wow! Her response hit me in the heart with such sadness that I'm sure she noticed it. I guess I was more shocked at the fact that this perspective came from a 15 year old, one who I believed was too young to know what real love is, but one, regrettably, old enough to have her understanding of love defined by what she saw in her parents. Some couples don't realize that loving the other person is a daily choice. Sooner later the "warm-fuzzies" and goose bumps wear off, and we see the other person for who they are, not for what we want him/her to be for us. The same is true with our relationship with Jesus. When Jesus was describing the sacramental nature of eating his flesh and drinking his blood, he made, pardon the pun, no bones about it. His name means "Savior" and that's what he came to be and do. This is who he is; take it or leave it.

It is true: we stand in a relationship with God where we are free to walk away at any time. Still, the most disturbing aspect to me is that God will let us. God will allow us to turn our backs on Him and walk away. However, in those situations I don't believe God throws up His hands and is resolved to the fact that we are lost forever. If we believe this, we are fooling ourselves. I don't think God is called, according to Francis Thompson, *The Hound of Heaven* for nothing. Ever watch hounds chase a fox? They are relentless. Once on the scent, nothing distracts them- not water barriers, briars, brutal cold or night. No matter how cunning and clever the fox is, eventually the hounds catch up.

If you have ever walked away from God, please realize in this moment, God has not walked away from you. God is relentless, ever calling for you to return: " *Ah, fondest, blindest, weakest, I am He Whom thou seekest! Thou dravest love from thee, who dravest Me"* (Thompson, 1978). He is ever reminding us of His great love; ever holding out that offer of mercy, grace and forgiveness. In fact, the beauty is that these gifts can be all ours again if we would simply turn around and allow ourselves to be embraced by the nail-scarred hands of Jesus. So the next time you are tempted to tell God to take a hike, remember the words of Peter, *"Lord to whom shall we go? You have the words of eternal life."* Thanks again, Peter. I'm certain your words have kept many a Christian anchored to the steadfast love of God.

Exercise:

(1) Begin by sitting comfortably. Take several deep breaths. When you are ready, read John 6:53-69 aloud. Silently meditate on these words. Make a note, which words resonate within your heart and soul. What sentence or phrase gets your attention? Sit with these for several minutes. Perhaps you may choose to read *The Hound of Heaven* by Francis Thompson. What images come up for you as you reflect on God's faithful persistence in your life?

(2) As you re-read the passage, interact with the story. Reflect on the story and imagine your reaction to Jesus' words about his sacrificial death. What images or words come to mind when you hear Jesus say *"I tell you the truth, unless you eat the flesh of the Son of Man and drink his blood, you have no life in you. Whoever eats my flesh and drinks my blood has eternal life, and I will raise him up at the last day. For my flesh is real food and my blood is real drink. Whoever eats my flesh and drinks my blood remains in me and I in him. Just as the living Father has sent me and I live because of the Father, so the one who feeds on me will live because of me.* Ask yourself: What have been those times when my understanding in Jesus and his purpose and stretched my faith? Recall those times when you have been tempted to walk away from

Jesus. What feelings arise within when you contemplate that God would allow you the freedom to walk away?

(3) Re-read the passage. Ask God, "Where does this passage touch my life today? Where in my life do the words of Peter provide an anchor for my soul? How has understanding changed your life?"

(4) Finally, ask yourself, "What it is that God wants me to do now as a result of meditating on this passage? What shadow areas of my life do I need to embrace and see as opportunities for spiritual growth and maturity?"

The Hound of Heaven
Francis Thompson (1859-1907)

I fled Him, down the nights and down the days;
I fled Him, down the arches of the years;
I fled Him, down the labyrinthine ways
Of my own mind; and in the mist of tears
I hid from Him, and under running laughter.
Up visited hopes I sped; and shot, precipitated,
Adown Titanic glooms of chasmed fears,
From those strong Feet that followed,
Followed after. But with unhurrying chase,
And unperturbèd pace,

Deliberate speed, majestic instancy,
They beat – and a Voice beat
More instant than the Feet –
"All things betray thee,
Who betrayest Me."

I pleaded, outlaw-wise,
By many a hearted casement, curtained red,
Trellised with intertwining charities;
(For, though I knew His love who followèd,
Yet I was sore adread
Lest having Him, I must have naught beside)
But, if one little casement parted wide,
The gust of His approach would clash it to:
Fear wist not to evade, as Love wist to pursue.
Across the margent of the world I fled,
And troubled the gold gateways of the stars,
Smiting for shelter on their clangèd bars;
Fretted to dulcet jars
And silvern chatter the pale ports o' the moon.
I said to Dawn: Be sudden – to Eve: Be soon;
With thy young skiey blossoms heap me over
From this tremendous Lover –
Float thy vague veil about me,
Lest He see!

I tempted all His servitors, but to find
My own betrayal in their constancy,
In faith to Him their fickleness to me,
Their traitorous trueness, and their loyal deceit.
To all swift things for swiftness did I sue;
Clung to the whistling mane of every wind.
But whether they swept, smoothly fleet,
The long savannahs of the blue;
Or whether, Thunder-driven,
They clanged his chariot 'thwart a heaven,
Plashy with flying lightnings round the spurn o' their feet: –
Fear wist not to evade as Love wist to pursue.
Still with unhurrying chase, and unperturbèd pace,
Deliberate speed, majestic instancy,
Came on the following Feet, and a Voice above their beat –
"Naught shelters thee, who wilt not shelter Me."

I sought no more that after which I strayed
In face of man or maid;
But still within the little children's eyes
Seems something, something that replies,
Theyat least are for me, surely for me!
I turned me to them very wistfully;
But just as their young eyes grew sudden fair
With dawning answers there,
Their angel plucked them from me by the hair.

"Come then, ye other children, Nature's — share
With me" (said I) "your delicate fellowship;
Let me greet you lip to lip,
Let me twine with you caresses,
Wantoning
With our Lady-Mother's vagrant tresses,
Banqueting
With her in her wind-walled palace,
Underneath her azured daïs,
Quaffing, as your taintless way is,
From a chalice
Lucent-weeping out of the dayspring."
So it was done:
In their delicate fellowship was one —
Drew the bolt of Nature's secrecies.
Iknew all the swift importings
On the wilful face of skies;
I knew how the clouds arise
Spumèd of the wild sea-snortings;
All that's born or dies
Rose and drooped with; made them shapers
Of mine own moods, or wailful or divine;
With them joyed and was bereaven.
I was heavy with the even,
When she lit her glimmering tapers
Round the day's dead sanctities.

I laughed in the morning's eyes.
I triumphed and I saddened with all weather,
Heaven and I wept together,
And its sweet tears were salt with mortal mine;
Against the red throb of its sunset-heart
I laid my own to beat,
And share commingling heat;
But not by that, by that, was eased my human smart.
In vain my tears were wet on Heaven's grey cheek.
For ah! we know not what each other says,
These things and I; in sound Ispeak —
Their sound is but their stir, they speak by silences.
Nature, poor stepdame, cannot slake my drouth;
Let her, if she would owe me,
Drop yon blue bosom-veil of sky, and show me
The breasts o' her tenderness:
Never did any milk of hers once bless
My thirsting mouth.
Nigh and nigh draws the chase,
With unperturbèd pace,
Deliberate speed, majestic instancy;
And past those noisèd Feet
A voice comes yet more fleet —
"Lo! naught contents thee, who content'st not Me."

Naked I wait Thy love's uplifted stroke!
My harness piece by piece Thou hast hewn from me,
And smitten me to my knee;
I am defenceless utterly.
I slept, methinks, and woke,
And, slowly gazing, find me stripped in sleep.
In the rash lustihead of my young powers,
I shook the pillaring hours
And pulled my life upon me; grimed with smears,
I stand amid the dust o' the mounded years —
My mangled youth lies dead beneath the heap.
My days have crackled and gone up in smoke,
Have puffed and burst as sun-starts on a stream.
Yea, faileth now even dream
The dreamer, and the lute the lutanist;
Even the linked fantasies, in whose blossomy twist
I swung the earth a trinket at my wrist,
Are yielding; cords of all too weak account
For earth with heavy griefs so overplussed.
Ah! is Thy love indeed
A weed, albeit an amaranthine weed,
Suffering no flowers except its own to mount?
Ah! must
Designer infinite! —
Ah! must Thou char the wood ere Thou canst limn with it?
My freshness spent its wavering shower i' the dust;

And now my heart is as a broken fount,

Wherein tear-drippings stagnate, spilt down ever

From the dank thoughts that shiver

Upon the sighful branches of my mind.

Such is; what is to be?

The pulp so bitter, how shall taste the rind?

I dimly guess what Time in mists confounds;

Yet ever and anon a trumpet sounds

From the hid battlements of Eternity;

Those shaken mists a space unsettle, then

Round the half-glimpsèd turrets slowly wash again.

But not ere him who summoneth

I first have seen, enwound

With glooming robes purpureal, cypress-crowned;

His name I know, and what his trumpet saith.

Whether man's heart or life it be which yields

Thee harvest, must Thy harvest-fields

Be dunged with rotten death?

Now of that long pursuit

Comes on at hand the bruit;

That Voice is round me like a bursting sea:

"And is thy earth so marred,

Shattered in shard on shard?

Lo, all things fly thee, for thou fliest Me!

Strange, piteous, futile thing!

Wherefore should any set thee love apart?
Seeing none but I makes much of naught" (He said),
"And human love needs human meriting:
How hast thou merited —
Of all man's clotted clay the dingiest clot?
Alack, thou knowest not
How little worthy of any love thou art!
Whom wilt thou find to love ignoble thee,
Save Me, save only Me?
All which I took from thee I did but take,
Not for thy harms,
But just that thou might'st seek it in My arms.
All which thy child's mistake
Fancies as lost, I have stored for thee at home:
Rise, clasp My hand, and come!"
Halts by me that footfall:
Is my gloom, after all,
Shade of His hand, outstretched caressingly?
"Ah, fondest, blindest, weakest,
I am He Whom thou seekest!
Thou dravest love from thee, who dravest Me."

Chapter 10

"Taking Hold of Something Better"
Matthew 19:23-30, Luke 18:18-30

*T*hen Jesus turned to them and said, "I tell you the truth, it is hard for a rich man to enter the kingdom of heaven. Again I tell you, it is easier for a camel to go through the eye of a needle than for a rich man to enter the kingdom of God." When the disciples heard this, they were greatly astonished and asked, "Who then can be saved?" Jesus looked at them and said, "With man this is impossible, but with God all things are possible." Peter answered him, "We have left everything to follow you! What then will there be for us?" Jesus said to them, I tell you the truth, at the renewal of all things, when the Son of Man sits on his glorious throne, you who have followed me will also sit on the twelve thrones, judging the twelve tribes of Israel. And everyone who has left houses or brothers or sisters or father or mother or children*

or fields for my sake will receive a hundred times as much and will inherit eternal life. But many who are first will be last, and many who are last will be first."

I once asked my students to describe the first time they were aware of following a spiritual path? Please note that I did not say religious path. A spiritual path is indeed different from a religious path in many ways. For some people, a religious path implies a vocation, such as pursuing ordination, vows of religious consecration, etc. A spiritual path, on the other hand, paints a broader picture of our search for meaning and purpose in our relationship with God or the divine. The students' answers were interesting. One person described his spirituality as taking a trip: *"Although you have a map that outlines what roads to take, and how long it might take you, you still cannot plan for some unforeseen dangers along the way, such as detours, accidents and construction."* Another person described her journey as something she has learned from watching others; as if she was following the trail marked by those who went before her. She said she often struggled in her faith because she would become so preoccupied with whether or not she was doing her spiritual practices correctly rather than finding personal fulfillment. Another student described his spiritual journey as something he doesn't remember as having an exact starting point; just something that he believed he was always on.

Indeed, there are many ways to describe a spiritual journey. Whether people believe their spiritual journey is like following a trail with twists and turns or a roadmap of many miles, each path is unique. The differences can be attributed to a number of reasons: First of all, not all of us become aware of God's voice at the same time in our lives. For some, childhood memories are filled with an awareness of God's presence. Such children may have been taught how to pray at an early age or attended more formal religious classes. Others may not have been aware of God's presence until later in life when they reexamined their priorities. Still, others may have become aware of God, following a family tragedy when people rallied around them with an outpouring of prayers and support. Another reason why each person may understand the spiritual journey differently is due to the fact that we all come from different backgrounds, cultures, and experiences. Even if we have had similar experiences (e.g., as births, graduations, marriages, divorces, and death of loved ones, etc.), we certainly do not interpret these events in the same way.

A tool people often use today to help them reflect on their spiritual journey is called a Labyrinth. In ancient times, people used to make pilgrimages to holy sites and lands as part of their spiritual journey towards self-transcendence. Many people continue this practice today. However, for people who cannot afford to travel to these holy sites, labyrinths have substituted as a walking path of contemplative prayer to God. Labyrinths combine the imagery of the circle and the spiral — both of which represent a journey to our own spiritual center and back again out into the world. Many people who walk labyrinths often experience a feeling they describe as grace, peace or holiness in their spirit as they are able to release pent up emotions they have carried inside. Others use their walking meditation as a means of reflecting how far they have spiritually matured, as well as realizing how far they have yet to go. Rev. Dr. Lauren Artress, Veriditas, of the Bon Secours Spiritual Center in Marriottsville, Maryland states, *"Walking the labyrinth clears the mind and gives insight into the spiritual journey. It urges action. It calms people in the throes of life transitions. It helps them see their lives in the context of a path - a pilgrimage. They realize that they are not human beings on a spiritual path but spiritual beings on a human path."*

I'm not sure if Peter ever walked a labyrinth contemplating how far he had come in his faith. Yet, one thing is sure; he wanted Jesus to note this. One of the things that strikes me about Peter's reaction to Jesus in this passage is the panic I can almost hear in his voice. Astonished and redfaced, the alarms go off inside of Peter: *"Lord, have you noticed (or even appreciate) all that we have done for you? All that we have left behind? We know this isn't a three-day retreat and then back to work. We have left everything and everyone to follow you!"* Many of us may also experience this level of exasperation when we think that others do not appreciate the sacrifices we make, or when we want to be reassured that our efforts will pay off.

Again, I believe we can identify with Peter because of our need to understand the nature of "cause and effect" in society. Perhaps you remember learning in Physics' class Sir Issac Newton's Third Law of Motion that states *"for every action, there's an equal and opposite reaction."* We might say it another way: *"If this and such happens, then this will likely occur."* Yet, can this same logic apply to our relationship with God? I don't think so. In fact, it's more of an illusion to think that we can manipulate God in this way. For example, without ever realizing it, many of us often treat God as a slot-machine: *"If we do this, then God will do that. We will serve God, but only after we have a guarantee that things will work out for us, as well as not looking foolish in the process. Furthermore, just in case nobody else is keeping track of what we have sacrificed, lost, or surrendered along the way, we can always remind God that He owes us by keeping track of all of life's dues we have paid."*

While it is true that thousands of people have left homes and families, excellent paying jobs, even more, to follow Christ, we tend to place so much emphasis on the *content* instead of the *process.* In other words, the goal of following Jesus is not so much the reward at the end. Indeed, this is not to minimize the wonderful promises we have in Scripture of eternal life with Christ. However, the goal of Christian discipleship is on the process, that is transformation into the image of Christ (Ephesians 4:11-13). For Peter, his focus was initially on the *content* of his spiritual path with Jesus. Yet in his preoccupation with the details of what he has forsaken, he forgot that in humble service toward others, his spiritual transformation was occurring moment by moment. Eventually, Peter did get it. We know this because later he writes:

Praise be to the God and Father of our Lord Jesus Christ. In his great mercy he has given us new birth into a living hope through the resurrection of Jesus Christ from the dead, and into an inheritance that can never perish, spoil or fade—kept in heaven for you. . . (1 Peter 1:3-4)

It's being conformed to the image of Jesus that takes time. After all, in the parable of the Sheep and the Goats (Mathew 25:31-46) wasn't the "reward" based on continued faithfulness? Far too many Christians in today's society are so preoccupied with what's in it for them that they forget that discipleship is not based on what we can get, but rather *what we can give; how can we serve?* The language of service with humility is unfortunately all but void in contemporary Christianity. Yet, it is often through service to others in need whereby people encounter life-changing moments of God's love and grace through the compassionate hearts and hands of those whom Christ has touched. Daily we wrestle with questions such as: *How have I served others today? What gifts and graces has God equipped me with to bless others? Who has God placed in my life to love and serve?* These are the questions that compel us to transcend our lives in order to fulfill lives of meaningful service.

Fr. Anthony DeMello (1984) tells a story about a wise man, who had reached the outskirts of a village and had settled down under a tree for the night, when all of a sudden a villager came running up to him and cried, *"The stone, the stone, give me the precious stone!" "What stone?"* asked the wise man. *"Last night, God appeared to me in a dream,'* said the villager, *"and told me that if I went to the outskirts of the village at dusk I would find a wise man who would give me a precious stone that would make me rich forever."* The wise man rummaged in his bag and pulled out a stone. *"He probably meant this one,"* he said, as he handed the stone over to the villager. *"I found it on a forest path some days ago. You can certainly have it."* The man looked at the stone in wonder. It was a diamond; probably the largest diamond in the whole world, for it was as large as a person's head! He took the diamond and walked away. However, all night the villager tossed in his bed unable to sleep. The next day, at the crack of dawn, he ran back to the wise man and said,

"Give me the wealth that makes it possible for you to give this diamond so easily."

With every person Christ met, there was an implicit, and sometimes explicit, challenge to let go of the former, in order to take hold of something better. Ironically, this is not a one-time call. Daily we are confronted with decisions to grasp things which either hinder or nurture the transforming work of the gospel in our lives. The "goal" then is to trust the process of the good work God has begun, and will continue in us to completion, until the day of Christ.

Exercise:

(1) Begin by sitting comfortably. Take several deep breaths. When you are ready, read Matthew 19:23-30 and Luke 18:26-30 aloud. Silently meditate on these words. Make a note, which words resonate within your heart and soul. What sentence or phrase gets your attention? Sit with these for several minutes.

If you have access to a labyrinth, you may use this prayer from Jean Sonnenberg for reflection:

O God of many paths, I stand before you in this labyrinth today, metaphor of my journey to you. In the Western world I have been taught that "the shortest distance between two points is a straight line," and being an impatient person, I am uncomfortable waiting. I have often modeled my journey to you on the straight line. But you, God of infinite patience, have shown me that there is another path, a curved path. On this path, my anticipation is heightened as I approach the center, only to be led out again to the periphery. But this path more closely resembles life itself. On this path, if I just put one foot in front of the other, it may seem at times as if I am not approaching my goal, while in fact, I am drawing closer all the time. But you are a God of surprises and mystery, and I don't control the path. The labyrinth is a symbol of my surrender to mystery, trusting, not knowing for certain, that the path which curves in and out again ultimately leads to the Center, which is You.

Bon Secours Labyrinth, Marriottsville, Maryland

(2) As you re-read the passage, interact with the story. Reflect on Jesus' words and imagine your reaction? How is it similar to Peter's? How would you describe your spiritual path with God? A road-trip containing twists and turns? Following a trail blazed by others? Perhaps you have another way of describing your walk with God.

(3) Re-read the passage. Ask God, "Where does this passage touch my life today? Where in my life do the words of Peter touch me? How have I been preoccupied with the content of my journey with God that you may hve overlooked the process God has been working in you? How has understanding changed your life?"

(4) Finally, ask yourself, "What it is that God wants me to do now as a result of meditating on this passage? What shadow areas of my life do I need to embrace and see as opportunities for spiritual growth and maturity?"

Chapter 11

"Sifting Through the Bold Statements"
Matthew 26:31-35, Mark 14:27-31,
Luke 22:31-34, John 13:31-38

*T*he Jesus told them, "This very night you all will fall away on account of me, for it is written: 'I will strike the shepherd, and the sheep of the flock will be scattered.' But after I have risen, I will go ahead of you into Galilee." Peter replied, "Even if all fall away on account of you, I never will." "I tell you the truth," Jesus answered, "This very night, before the rooster crows, you will disown me three times." But Peter declared, "Even if I have to die with you, I will never disown you." And all the other disciples said the same.

"Simon, Simon, Satan has asked to sift you as wheat. But I have prayed for you, Simon, that your faith may not fail.

And when you have turned back, strengthen your brothers."
But he (Peter) replied, "Lord, I am ready to go with you to
prison and to death." Luke 22:31-33

Within the past years, one of God's greatest inventions
has hit the market: Ready-made cookie dough. All you have
to do is peel back the wrapping and place the individual balls
of dough on your cookie sheet and after 10 minutes in your
oven, you'll have hot, fresh cookies. Now I know some of
you out there right now are shaking your heads saying, *"If
you're not cracking eggs, you're not baking!"* True. Still,
God bless the people who make it easier for the rest of us. Of
course, ready-made cookie dough also eliminates the treat
of licking the beaters after mixing all the ingredients: a true
childhood rite of passage.

I remember the days when my mother owned one of those
old-style flour sifters. You remember the ones with the little
crank that would turn the whisk around and force the flour
through the wire mesh? The sifter my mother had was old
and somewhat rusty. Still, she loved to bake cookies or make
home-made noodles for stew. Since I wasn't old enough to
do anything else at the time, it was my job to sift the flour.
My mother added the scoops of flour and I would start to
crank. Sometimes the cranking would go smoothly, but most
often I would end up tapping the side of the tin to sift the
remaining flour. Now, the whole purpose behind sifting is

not only to create a lighter-textured flour, but also to separate the impurities; those hardened pieces that were then thrown away. To the naked eye you cannot tell those pieces are in the bag of flour. It's only during the sifting process that you really see what doesn't belong.

In the Gospel of Luke, just prior to predicting Peter's denial, Jesus tells Peter that this is what Satan has asked to do to him. . .to pass him through the "mesh" and see what he is really made of. As typical of Peter, we sense a spark of arrogance in his tone when he responds, *"Don't worry Lord, if everyone else turns away, I'll never deny you. I will follow you to the death."* I wonder if Peter ever met Shadrach, Meshach and Abednego? (Daniel 3) Their story is certainly one of faithful courage in the face of death. Yet, for most of us we might struggle with what we might do or say in the "heat of the moment." In other words, it's one thing to be confident and certain of your faith when things are going well, but what about when you're facing a furnace? Our faith can be strong when the pantry if full, but what about when we're facing empty shelves?

We also tend to fall into this trap when we watch movies. The characters are portrayed to possess super-sleuth skills, or be larger than life as we look over their shoulders and admire their bravery. Too often we live vicariously through others and forget that they bleed like us when they are cut. In reading this passage, what should be obvious to us is that you would think Peter would have known better after all that he experienced with Christ. Imagine, he actually thinks he knows himself better than God does. (Sure glad we don't behave this way!) Perhaps being unable to imagine the fate that awaited Jesus was why Peter puffed out his chest and said what he did.

The sifting process is not a pleasant one; in fact, it is downright painful. Scholars and theologians refer to this as the process of refining. When a smith wanted to refine precious metal such as gold or silver, he would heat the metal to liquid and as the impurities would rise to the surface, he would then scoop off the dross. This process would be repeated until the metal was pure. However, today most of our metal in jewelry is made up of an alloy: that is, two or more elements which are combined to add strength and durability to our watches, bracelets and rings. The same is true when a grain is sifted. The process sifts to remove that which is impure so that what remains is pure.

In our lives, we can also refer to this process as God's way of removing the impurities in our lives until our hearts are refined or sifted. If we are honest with ourselves, we would admit that we want is purity in our lives; purity of heart, thought and speech. As much as we want it, we tend to deny or at least overlook the fact that those qualities come only from sifting times when our faith is tested or patience is tried. Most often we do not recognize the sifting process while we're going through a difficult situation. It's only during times of hindsight that we can look back and see the hand of God in our lives, producing the results. Many people often describe their periods of intense sifting as their "dark night of the soul." While this is a popular belief, St. John's "dark night" more accurately represents those moments when he felt trapped in a spiritual desert, all the while his soul ached for intimacy with God. In her unique translation of this mystical classic, Mirabai Starr (2002) cautions us not to take these moments lightly: *"For John, the dark night is an excruciating but necessary step of the spiritual journey wherein all familiar spiritual feelings and concepts of God dry up and fall into obscurity, leaving the seeker in a state of profound emptiness. This is the true beginning of the path to union in love with the Divine."*

In the days that followed the attacks of *September 11*, I listened carefully to the analogies of the bombing used by the elderly as compared to those used by younger generations. The younger generations seemed more insecure in their feelings and quite uncertain about the future. Ironically, this stemmed from the fact that they had nothing to compare the attacks to in their lifetime. On the other hand, the elderly appeared upset at the news, but had an underlying core of resolve. It's as if they had been through something like this before. In fact they had. It was called D-Day and the attack on Pearl Harbor. The generations that lived through World War

I, The Great Depression and World War II had an unshake-
able determination that they would get through the present
uncertainty because of how they had been sifted. You know
what amazed me the most about them? The fact that they
brought comfort to so many others, not by the words they
spoke, but by what you could see in their eyes. It was as
if they were living out Jesus' words, *"And when you come
back, strengthen your brothers (and sisters)."*

Do you think Peter quickly forgot this lesson? Not a
chance! Instead, that lesson shaped the rest of his life. It
can shape ours, too. It doesn't take much these days to find
a person who is in need of encouragement, strength and
peace. It is a shame that too many do not value our elderly
for their lived-experiences and wisdom. Perhaps we could
save ourselves a lot of sleepless nights and worry lines in
the process! How will our children and grandchildren and
generations yet to be born know that God is faithful to the
process unless we are faithful in living by example? For
Peter, being sifted wasn't the end of the story (ours neither),
because Jesus also held out a wonderful promise for him
and us: *"And when you come back, strengthen your brothers
(and sisters)."* Indeed, no matter what we face, whether
intense suffering or the intense longing for God in that spiritual desert, there will be times when the clouds part, springs
of water will flow, and a night spent in tears will lead to
joy in the morning. It's no small detail that Jesus' promise

occurs during Holy Week. Jesus was already looking beyond his arrest, his trial, his crucifixion, and resurrection. Jesus was looking to Pentecost, a time when indeed Peter would strengthen his brothers and sisters with the powerful declaration of salvation made available through God's grace in Christ Jesus.

Exercise:

(1) Begin by sitting comfortably. Take several deep breaths. When you are ready, read Matthew 26:31-35, Mark 14:27-31, Luke 22:31-34, John 13:31-38 aloud. Silently meditate on these words. Make a note, which words resonate within your heart and soul. What sentence or phrase gets your attention? Sit with these for several minutes. Perhaps you may choose to read and reflect on poem of *The Dark Night of the Soul* by St. John of the Cross. If so, remember those times in your life when you felt like being a spiritual desert, intensely longing for God. What emotions stir in you as a result of reflecting on these experiences? What emotions stir in you once you discovered that intimacy with God once again?

(2) As you re-read the passage, interact with the story. Reflect on the story and imagine your reaction to Jesus' words to you. What feelings emerge when you realize

that Jesus allows, often initiates, the purification of your heart? What have been those times in your life when you have been sifted and tried? What have been some of the issues in your life that have come to the surface? What issues remain?

(3) Re-read the passage. Ask God, "Where does this passage touch my life today? Where in my life do the words of Peter strike a cord in me? How has this understanding changed your life?" "How can God use me to strengthen others?"

(4) Finally, ask yourself, "What is it that God wants me to do now as a result of meditating on this passage? What shadow areas of my life do I need to embrace and see as opportunities for spiritual growth and maturity?"

The Dark Night of the Soul
(Stanzas of the Soul)
St. John of the Cross (1542-1591)

One dark night,
fired with love's urgent longings
- ah, the sheer grace! -
I went out unseen,
my house being now all stilled.

In darkness, and secure,
by the secret ladder, disguised,
- ah, the sheer grace! -
in darkness and concealment,
my house being now all stilled.

On that glad night,
in secret, for no one saw me,
nor did I look at anything,
with no other light or guide
than the one that burned in my heart.

This guided me
more surely than the light of noon
to where he was awaiting me
- him I knew so well -
there in a place where no one appeared.

O guiding night!
O night more lovely than the dawn!
O night that has united
the Lover with his beloved,
transforming the beloved in her Lover.

continued

Upon my flowering breast
which I kept wholly for him alone,
there he lay sleeping,
and I caressing him
there in a breeze from the fanning cedars.

When the breeze blew from the turret,
as I parted his hair,
it wounded my neck
with its gentle hand,
suspending all my senses.

I abandoned and forgot myself,
laying my face on my Beloved;
all things ceased; I went out from myself,
leaving my cares
forgotten among the lilies.

Chapter 12

John 13:1-17
A Tale of Two Basins, Tells The Tale

*I*t was just before the Passover Feast. Jesus knew that the time had come for him to leave this worldand go to the Father. Having loved his own, he now showed them the full extent of his love. The evening meal was being served and the devil had already prompted Judas Iscariot, son of Simon, to betray Jesus. Jesus knew that the Father had put all things under his power, and that he had come from God and was returning to God; so he got up from the meal, took off his outer clothing, and wrapped a towel around his waist. After that, he poured water into a basin and began to wash his disciples' feet, drying them with the towel that was wrapped around him.

He came to Simon Peter, who said to him, "Lord, are you going to wash my feet?" Jesus replied, "You do not realize now what I am doing, but later you will understand." "No," said Peter, "you shall never wash my feet." Jesus answered, "You do not realize now what I am doing, but later you will understand." "Then, Lord," Simon Peter replied, "not just my feet but my hands and my head as well!" Jesus answered, "A person who has had a bath needs only to wash his feet; his whole body is clean. And you are clean, though not every one of you." For he knew who was going to betray him, and that was why he said not every one was clean.

When he had finished washing their feet, he put on his clothes and returned to his place. "Do you understand what I have done for you?" he asked them. "You call me 'Teacher' and 'Lord,' and rightly so, for that is what I am. Now that I, your Lord and Teacher, have washed your feet, you also should wash one another's feet. I have set you an example that you should do as I have done for you. I tell you the truth, no servant is greater than his master, nor is a messenger greater than the one who sent him. Now that you know these things, you will be blessed if you do them."

In the opening monologue of the movie *Forrest Gump*, Tom Hanks' character recalls his mother's words about shoes: "*My mama always said you could learn a lot from other people's shoes; where they've been. . .* (Pointing to the shoes of the woman sitting next to him on the bench). *Those look like comfortable shoes. I wish I had a paitr of shoes like them. I bet you could walk all day in shoes like that.*" To which the lady sitting next to Forrest Gump replies, *"My feet hurt."* Feet do hurt, especially if you have been walking or standing all day. In fact, experts tell us that there are 26 bones, 33 joints, and more than 100 tendons, muscles, and ligaments in the human foot. Furthermore, foot pain can affect pain in the legs, hips, and back. What's even more astonishing is that the foot has more than 250,000 sweat glands. No wonder our mothers always told us to put on clean socks! In fact, the first thing most people do when they get home after a hard day of work is to take off their shoes!

Growing up I recall how my family loved to soak their feet in a basin of hot water and Epsom© salts. I still do this soothing ritual from time to time. In fact for me, contemplation seems to come naturally when I'm sitting with my feet, ankle deep in hot water. I often reflect on this passage in John's gospel, especially how at times, God uses ordinary things to carry on the work of transformation in my life. Moreover, it seemed that Jesus went out of his way to find the everyday, ordinary things in order to demonstrate his extraordinary grace. Take footwashing for example. In Jesus' day, footwashing was performed by a servant on guests as they entered the home. This simple act of washing away dirt and grime spoke volumes in terms of a host's hospitality. Therefore, it must have been quite a shock to see Jesus perform a servant's duty at the supper he was hosting. After all, Jesus emphasized how much he looked forward to spending that particular Passover Meal with his disciples. Surely there had to have been at least one servant among them!

What strikes me the most in this passage is the dialogue between Jesus and Peter reagrding another transforming lesson Peter will learn from having his feet washed by Jesus. *He came to Simon Peter, who said to him, "Lord, are you going to wash my feet?" Jesus replied, "You do not realize now what I am doing, but later you will understand."* True, Peter did not understand what Jesus was doing. Perhaps his question revealed his embarrasement that none of the disciples, including himself, offered to perform such a menial task. Perhaps he was ashamed that his teacher, who performed miracles by healing the sick and raising the dead, was now in a bent over position, cleaning the dirt and grime from between Peter's toes. I like to think that through his deep love and humble service, Jesus had given the disciples a wonderful gift of grace that Peter realized only after Jesus' arrest and trial. For example, one Lenten Season I remember watching a re-enactment of a possible dialogue between Judas and Peter if they both returned to the upper room following Jesus' arrest. By examining the motivations of each man, the audience was continually reminded of this question: *"Which is more difficult for us to forgive: betrayal or denial? Which sin is worse in our opinion?"* I'm certain both Judas and Peter were shocked just how easily Jesus was taken away within a few hours after the meal. After all, they may have recalled the many times before how Jesus walked right through angry crowds untouched. We might then imagine each man standing in the empty room with a heavy heart, realizing what sins he and the other committed: Judas, the one who betrayed Jesus for thirty pieces of silver by bringing the soldiers to arrest him; and Peter, the one who denied ever knowing Jesus in the first place. What made this play so profound was that each man had the audacity to point his finger at the other and hurl accusations.

Since Judas seemed to be preoccupied with power, I wonder if Peter reminded him what true power was all about? Did he remind him about all the miracles he saw Jesus perform? What about turning boy's lunch into a meal that fed 5,000 people? (Matthew 14:13-21) What about the time when a woman was healed from her discharge of blood just by touching the hem of Jesus' garment? (Luke 8:43-48) What about Jesus raising Lazarus from the dead? (John 11:38-44). Yet perhaps no sooner these words left Peter's lips than he realized how they applied to him. Since Peter seemed to enjoy being close to Jesus, I wonder if Judas reminded him what true intimacy was all about? Did he remind him about all of the miracles he saw Jesus perform? What about standing on the mountain with Jesus as he was transfigured before Peter's eyes? (Matthew 17:1-8) What about the time when Jesus pulled Peter out of the sea as he was sinking?

(John 6:16-24) What about the time when Peter blurted out, *"You are the Christ, the holy one of God!"*? (Mark 8:27-30) *"Which is harder for us to forgive? Betrayal or denial? Which sin is worse in our opinion?"*

Earlier during the Last Supper, Jesus told his disciples these things would happen. Each one answered, *"Surely not I, Lord?" I would never do that. Surely you're talking about someone else."* Yet, how could they be so certain? How could they know what a person's response will be before something happens? Perhaps Judas was off to the side, contemplating what he would do with the money for handing Jesus over to the authorities. Maybe he would have used that money for the poor, or maybe he might have helped himself? Either way, Judas may have thought Jesus would have done what he always did: walk right through the crowd, but not this time. This time Jesus was arrested. Remarkedly, Peter was there too, probably sitting very close to Jesus. Yet, Peter's words echo in our ears, *"Though everyone else deserts you, Lord, I will never fall away! Even if it means death!"*

How did Jesus know these two men would do such things? Perhaps Jesus knows our true nature. Perhaps Jesus knows that when the going gets tough, we are more likely to get going in the opposite direction. Funny how quickly are words and actions reveal what lies beneath the surface of our hearts. We say things at the time that seem pretty reasonable, given the state of mind we're in, but how often do our words come back to haunt us? The truth is anyone we are capable of betraying and denying Jesus. In fact, many people I've counseled are haunted by the memory of having either denied or betrayed Jesus at one time or another. Still, in their desire to live their lives for Christ, they may be baffled how actions of betrayal and denial can occupy the same place in their hearts as love and devotion to God? In his book, *Can You Drink From the Cup?*, Henri Nouwen (2006) a Dutch priest and theologian, compared the irony of the cup Jesus was about to metaphorically drink through his suffering and death, with contemplating the condition of our hearts. By examining how Jesus embrace both the sorrow (his passion and death on the cross) and joy (the salvation of our souls through his resurrection) of this cup, so too we are called to embrace the sorrow and joy in our lives. In other words, both heartbreak and celebration come from the same cup, the same heart.

To reinforce this lesson, Jesus gave the disciples the gift of humble service, as well as the responsibility to go and serve others. *"Now that I, your Lord and Teacher, have washed your feet, you also should wash one another's feet. I have set you an example that you should do as I have done for you."* The spirit in which Jesus washed his disciple's feet struck the tone of true discipleship that seeks to serve others with humility. Whatever the task, whether it is being a hospice worker who holds the hand of a dying person, or one who provides food, shelter and clothing to those in need, humble service always provides those who are being served the opportunity to respond to God's grace. Although Jesus knew suffering, pain and death awaited him, that night it was all about the disciples' need to understand the full extent of Jesus' love. True ordinariness, in the image of a servant's heart, is indeed tangible holiness (Wicks, 2007).

Yes, the disciples still had a lot to learn. So do we. After all, servanthood is a decision, a daily choice. We will be confronted with decisions as physical, emotional and spiritual needs arise. Will we serve or will we pretend it is someone else's problem? The foot-washing basin was not the only basin used in the gospels. There was a second basin mentioned, the one Pilate used not to wash the feet of others, but his own hands. After Jesus' initial arrest and trial before the Jewish ruling council called the Sanhedrin, he was then taken to Pilate, Govenor of Judea, and demanded he be crucified. Unsure of which course of action to take, Pilate consulted with his wife, who assured him that Jesus was indeed a righteous man. This only increased the conflict within Pilate's heart. What should he do? As the crowd escalated their call for Jesus' crucifixion, Pilate took a basin and literally washed his hands of what to do with Jesus (Matthew 27:1-24). Amazing, one who had the power to set Jesus free or condemn him to death, showed his indifference through it all. Like Lady MacBeth who cried, *"Out, damn'd spot! Out, I say! One; two: why, then 'tis time to do't,"* Pilate chose to wash his hands of Jesus' blood, but his own guilt remained stained in his fingerprints. Interestingly, the blood of Christ which would have cleansed his heart "making his sins whiter than snow," had become the basin which contained his guilt.

Two basins. Two responses. One speaks of humble service to others. The other speaks of shirked responsibility. One looks at the dirty water and claims forgiveness and grace through the washing away of sins. The other looks at the self-reflection and claims emptiness. If you have difficulty knowing which one to choose at times, consider this parable:

A holy man was having a conversation with the Lord one day and said, "Lord, I would like to know what Heaven and Hell are like." The Lord led the holy man to two doors. He opened one of the doors and the holy man looked in. In the middle of the room was a large round table. In the middle of the table was a large pot of stew which smelled delicious and made the holy man's mouth water. But the people sitting around the table were thin and sickly. They appeared to be famished. They were holding spoons with very long handles that were strapped to their arms and each found it possible to reach into the pot of stew and take a spoonful, but because the handle was longer than their arms, they could not get the spoons back into their mouths. The holy man shuddered at the sight of their misery and suffering. The Lord said, 'You have seen Hell.' They then went to the next room and opened the door. It was exactly the same as the first one. There was the large round table with the large pot of stew which made the holy man's mouth water. The people were equipped with the same long-handled spoons, but here the people were well nourished and plump, laughing and talking. The holy man said, "I don't understand." "It is simple" said the Lord, "In this place the people have learned to feed one another."

Exercise:

(1) Begin by sitting comfortably. Take several deep breaths. When you are ready, read John 13:1-17 aloud. If you like, you may also use this exercise to read aloud the words of Matthew 27:1-24 and the Apostle's Creed. Silently meditate on these words. Make a note, which words resonate within your heart and soul. What sentence or phrase gets your attention? Sit with these for several minutes.

(2) As you re-read the passage, interact with the stories. Reflect on these stories and imagine yourself as Peter watching Jesus wash your feet. What do you hear/see/smell/feel as Jesus approaches you? What comes to mind when you hear Jesus say, *"Now that I, your Lord and*

Teacher, have washed your feet, you also should wash one another's feet. I have set you an example that you should do as I have done for you."

(3) Re-read the passage. Ask God, "Where does this passage touch my life today?" If you choose to do a deeper meditation, compare the two basins in these passages. Fill a basin with water and imagine how you have served others in the past, as well imagine how you may have "washed your hands of things?" What feelings arise in you knowing that Jesus has washed away your sins? What kind of resistance arises in you when you think about your role as servant? What underlying needs are met in you as you serve others? Do other people have to appreciate what you've done for them? What would Jesus do or say regarding the excuses you make? How does your present level of discipleship compare to Jesus' examples?

(4) Finally, ask yourself, "What it is that God wants me to do as a result of meditating on this passage?" "Is there an area in my life that I need to trust God more with?" "How can I further ground my service to others in humility?

The Apostle's Creed

I believe in God the Father Almighty, Maker of heaven and earth: And in Jesus Christ his only Son, our Lord; who was conceived by the Holy Ghost, born of the virgin Mary, suffered under Pontius Pilate, was crucified, dead, and buried; he descended into hell; the third day he rose again from the dead; he ascended into heaven, and sitteth on the right hand of God the Father Almighty; from thence he shall come to judge the quick and the dead. I believe in the Holy Ghost; the holy catholic (universal) church; the communion of saints; the forgiveness of sins; the resurrection of the body; and the life everlasting. Amen

Chapter 13

"Cursing a Blue Streak"
Luke 22:54-62, Matthew 26:69-75,
Mark 14:66-72, John 18:15-18, 25-27

*T*hen seizing him (Jesus), they led him away and took him to the high priest. Peter followed at a distance. But when they had kindled a fire in the middle of the courtyard and had sat down together, Peter sat down with them. A servant girl saw him seated there in the firelight. She looked closely at him and said, "This man was with him." But he (Peter) denied it. "Woman, I don't know him," he said. A little later someone else saw him and said, "You are also one of them." "Man, I am not!" Peter replied. About an hour later another asserted, "Certainly this fellow was with him, for he is a Galilean." Peter replied, "Man, I don't know what you're taking about!" Just as he was speaking, the rooster crowed. The Lord turned and looked straight at Peter. Then Peter remembered the word the Lord had spoken to him:

"Before the rooster crows today, you will disown me three times." And he (Peter) went outside and wept bitterly.

These days, companies invest thousands, if not millions, of dollars every year to secure their stores against theft by using time-locked safes, motion detectors, and elaborate alarm systems. To save costs, some department stores are notorious for having mirrors and surveillance cameras strategically located throughout their premises. Most people are not aware of the significance of these mirrors, other than to take a quick look at themselves to make sure their hair is straight or the clothes they try on look good from all angles. Attractive as this may sound, this is probably not their function. The main reason why department stores install mirrors in various locations is to deter shoplifting. That's right. Studies have shown that people are less likely to commit crimes if they know they're being watched. Sounds simple, but it works! Think about it: Even though we look in the mirror many times a day, there is something unsettling when somebody else points out our motivations and behavior by holding up a mirror to our face.

For this reason, I am convinced many people avoid going into therapy to work on personal issues. Whether it is symptoms of depression, anxiety, an inability to cope with stressful situations, or a more severe level of mental-health impairment, people are often oblivious to their shortcomings.

It may typically take family members or friends first to point out the problematic attitudes and behaviors repeatedly before the person sees the need for professional help. Unfortunately, between the time when their behavior becomes evident to others and the time it takes for them to make an appointment with a doctor or therapist, these persons may use all kinds of excuses: denial, blaming others, withdrawing or isolating themselves, projecting negative attitudes onto others, or acting out in passive-aggressive ways. It seems that the tighter they try to hold themselves together, the more their lives begin to crumble. For many, taking an honest look at themselves, let alone coming to grips with the harm they may have done to others, is just too painful.

Peter's denial of Jesus is recorded in all four gospels. Imagine, within a few short hours, Peter went from being a bold and courageous disciple, ready to lay down his life for Jesus, to an anxious and terrified commoner, denying any and all affiliations with him, all thanks to a servant girl and others who simply had inquisitive natures as they held up the proverbial mirror to Peter. Yet, out of all four gospels, only Luke (22: 60-62) provides us with one important detail that really drives home the emotional impact of Peter's actions:

> *Peter replied, "Man, I don't know what you're talking about!" Just as he was speaking, the rooster crowed. The Lord turned and looked straight at Peter. Then*

Peter remembered the word the Lord had spoken to him: "Before the rooster crows today, you will disown me three times." And he (Peter) went outside and wept bitterly.

I cannot imagine the pain and heartbreak Peter must have felt at that moment. The shame must have been unbearable! Not only did he bear the immense burden of sorrow seeing Jesus arrested and taken away, but also he would then realize that his own words condemned him. Just one look from Jesus must have shattered his heart. At that point, all Peter could do was turn away and hide.

I know what you're thinking. Right now, as you're reading this chapter, you're probably saying, *"Nope, that wouldn't be me. After all, that was another time and place. Besides, I'm not Peter. I know better."* Keep that in mind the next time you feel the sting in your heart when you're treated differently for being a Christian. Perhaps you have already experienced this treatment: the negative comments, the sneers and contemptuous looks, and perhaps threats of physical harm. If you haven't so far, you will. Just as Jesus told his disciples, the same words apply to all who love the Lord: *"If the world hates you, keep in mind that it hated me first . . . if they persecuted me, they will persecute you"* (John 15:18, 20). Remember, the closer you walk with Jesus the more likely it will be that you face persecution. Nobody enjoys persecution on any level, but perhaps the spiritual transformation that has begun in you just might be holding up a mirror to the world's face.

Just hours before Jesus' arrest and trial, Peter believed that even if everybody else grew a yellow streak down his/her back, the Lord could count on him to remain strong. He will be the one not only standing up for Jesus but also standing with him. I wonder. . .if the servant girl and others were on Peter's side that night, and assured him that he would be safe, would Peter have denied Christ? I don't know. We can only speculate. The events of Jesus' arrest and trial were rapidly unfolding before Peter's eyes. He may have thought that if the Romans could get to Jesus, they could easily get to him as well. Unfortunately, Peter didn't realize that it is only too human that when faced with a point of no return, we often look for an off-ramp.

This story reminds us that even the most devoted followers of Jesus can collapse under the weight of applied pressure, and collapse Peter does! His pain and disgrace is so great that he is reduced to tears. Nonetheless, what is often over-looked in this passage is the kind of tears Peter sheds. The New Testament Greek uses the word *klaio*, which means to sob heavily. These are not the same kind of tears Jesus shed in the famous verse in John 11:35 where he "wept" (*dakruo*) at the tomb of Lazarus. On the contrary, those tears of Jesus were simply the kind that slowly roll down our cheeks and that we could neatly dab with a tissue. However, these tears of Peter were uncontrollable, wailing, gut-wrenching, heart-breaking sobs. These gushing tears are the ones that force you to double-over in pain, and leave you exhausted when finished. Not too many people are quick to allow others to see this level of vulnerability from them. Perhaps this was why Peter left so abruptly.

Most people may not be aware of the anguish, anger and heartbreak that lies just below the surface of tears. Beginning counseling students often make the mistake of wanting to target the anger in a client's life, by introducing some form of anger management. This approach may be appropriate depending on the circumstances. However, I sometimes caution them that it might be too early in the counseling relationship for clients to address their anger issues without first realizing the cause of their anger. Instead, I teach students to listen first for what's underneath that anger or rage by asking themselves the following questions: *How do clients describe their anger? Are they (students) able to hear the sorrow and pain in the midst of angry words and actions? How have their clients been hurt? Who has hurt them? Where have their clients taken that pain and sorrow out into the world? How have the clients' relationships been affected by their anger? And so forth.* Sooner or later students recognize in their clients, layers of pain and sorrow from previous wounds that have yet to be healed.

In our society, it's not uncommon to turn on the television and hear about the latest incident of road-rage that ended in a fatality. The story typically involves a driver getting even with another driver who cut him off in traffic, honked at him for not paying attention when the light turned green, or criticized him for some other irresponsible behavior behind the wheel. I counseled a 50-something year old man named Sam for such actions. After his driver's license was suspended, he was required by the state transportation department to attend counseling for anger management related to his driving. When Sam and I met for the first time, I could tell why he was sent for counseling. He presented as nervous, irritable, and guarded. After some time, Sam told me his story of how anger and rage plagued him most of his life. Like most people having difficulty controlling their anger, Sam believed it was everybody else's fault. *"If only they wouldn't do things to make me mad!"* Yet, as he revealed more of his life, it occurred to me that Sam's anger took the classic form. It was signaling an unmet need and for Sam it was to guard him from pain. The anger was only a shield, a protection from further wounding. The thing Sam feared the most was being vulnerable. When Sam was a teenager he was attacked by several other boys in school. Because nobody came to his rescue, he felt completely unprotected; something he vowed he would never allow himself to feel again. As he grew older this vow was transferred to anyone who came close to making him feel defenseless, helpless or susceptible to danger. Therefore, when the driving habits or accidents of other people came too close to Sam, he reacted by lashing out in anger and rage. He wanted to make other drivers pay by striking in them fear and terror for arousing those feelings of vulnerability in him. Each week, I held up the mirror (metaphorically speaking) and gently allowed Sam to talk about his painful wounds from his youth. In a safe environment, Sam talked about his pain and humiliation after all these years, as well as to confront his feelings of living in a world in which a person has limited control over what may or may not occur.

Many of us often find ourselves vacillating between the past, present and future, i.e., what we were, who we are and what we would like to be. With my clients who are in this situation, I often use a technique taken from an ancient wedding tradition still observed by many villages in China today. Following the wedding ceremony, when the new bride is about leave with her husband and join his family, the bride's mother will give her a double-sided mirror. Her mother tells her that for the first half of the journey to her new home, she is to look at her face in the mirror and remember her past: where she has come from, her family, and what she leaves behind. At the half-way point of the journey, the new bride then turns the mirror over and looks at her face again. However, this time she is told to see herself in terms of the future: the entire time she will face as a wife, mother and perhaps grandmother. In the present moment, she is both what she has been and what she will be. Each day then is to be lived as who she is (Cunxin, 2003).

In a sense, life's journey is all about holding a double-sided mirror. On one side, we remember our experiences, the changes that have occurred and the lessons they have taught us. We also have times when we turn the mirror over and look to the future, seeing what we can become, antici-pating what's on the horizon. Nonetheless, we all stand in the present and need to be reminded that the most precious things in life do not come with a price-tag: The touch of a loved-one's hand, a smile, a kind word, feeling the coolness of a fall breeze, even the refreshing smell of a spring rain. If we look and listen closely enough with our hearts, we realize all of these experiences are not without their challenges, along with opportunities for personal growth. Socrates once said, *"The unexamined life is not worth living."* Interestingly, he said these words at his public trial in 399 BCE. He was being charged with the crime of heresy for encouraging others to challenge the accepted beliefs of the time and think for them-selves. By examining the world around them and discussing how to make the world a better place, people discovered that life became a more meaningful experience for all. For all of us, examining life first begins with the person in the mirror.

Exercise:

(1) Begin by sitting comfortably. Take several deep breaths. When you are ready, read Luke 22:54-62, Matthew 26:69-75, Mark 14:66-72, John 15-18, 25-27 aloud. Silently meditate on these words. Make a note, which words resonate within your heart and soul. What sentence or phrase gets your attention? Sit with these for several minutes.

(2) As you re-read the passage, interact with the story. Reflect on Luke's version of the story and imagine yourself as Peter when Jesus looks straight at you after you have committed sin. What feelings come up in you? Imagine if Jesus' eyes could speak, what would they say to you? What would you say to Jesus in that moment? Perhaps you might choose to hold a double-sided mirror in front of you. On one side, remember where you have been, your history, your sins and shortcomings, your accomplishments and celebrations, your life up to this moment. Reflect on these for a few moments. Then when you are ready, turn the mirror over and consider all that awaits you in the future: your opportunities for personal growth, how your life might be a blessing to others, wisdom gained from your experiences, those who you will love

and will love you. Take a moment and thank God for all that is being reflected in you and through you each day.

(3) Re-read the passage. Ask God, "Where does this passage touch my life today?" "How have I denied Jesus?" "How do I respond when the Holy Spirit's conviction feels like a mirror is being held to me to see who I really am?"

(4) Finally, ask yourself, "What is it that God wants me to do as a result of meditating on this passage?" "What areas of my life do I need to probe to discover untapped areas of faithfulness and perseverance in my life?"

Chapter 14

"The One Step Jesus Will Not Take"

John 21:1-19

*A*fterwards Jesus appeared again to his disciples, by the Sea of Tiberias. It happened this way: Simon Peter, Thomas (called Didymus), Nathanael from Cana in Galilee, the sons of Zebedee, and two other disciples were together. "I'm going out to fish," Simon Peter told them, and they said, "We'll go with you." So they went out and got into the boat, but that night they caught nothing. Early in the morning, Jesus stood on the shore, but the disciples did not realize that it was Jesus. He called out to them, "Friends, haven't you any fish?" "No," they answered. He said, "Throw your net on the right side of the boat and you will find some." When they did, they were unable to haul the net in because of the large number of fish.

Then the disciple whom Jesus loved said to Peter, "It is the Lord!" As soon as Simon Peter heard him say, "It is the Lord," he wrapped his outer garment around him (for he had taken it off) and jumped into the water. The other disciples followed in the boat, towing the net full of fish, for they were not far from shore, about a hundred yards. When they landed, they saw a fire of burning coals there with fish on it, and some bread. Jesus said to them, "Bring some of the fish you have just caught." Simon Peter climbed aboard and dragged the net ashore. It was full of large fish, 153, but even with so many the net was not torn. Jesus said to them, "Come and have breakfast." None of the disciples dared to ask him, "Who are you?" They knew it was the Lord. Jesus came and took bread and gave it to them, and did the same with the fish. This was now the third time Jesus appeared to his disciples after he was raised from the dead.

When they had finished eating, Jesus said to Simon Peter, "Simon, son of John, do you truly love me more than these?" "Yes Lord," he said, "you know that I love you." Jesus said, "Feed my lambs." Again Jesus said, "Simon son of John, do you truly love me?" He answered, "Yes, Lord, you know that I love you." Jesus said, "Take care of my sheep." The third time Jesus said to him, "Simon son of John, do you love me?" Peter was hurt because Jesus asked him a third time, "Do you love me?" He said, "Lord, you know all things; you know I love you." Jesus said, "Feed my sheep. I tell you the truth, when you were younger you dressed yourself an went where you wanted; but when you are old you will stretch out your hands, and someone else will dress you and lead you where you do not want to go." Jesus said this to indicate the kind of death by which Peter would glorify God. The he said to him, "Follow me!"

If you are like me, you are amazed at how church attendances swell on Easter Sunday. In fact, attendance doubles, sometimes even triples, leading up to and including the Easter celebration. Then, in the following weeks after Easter, attendance reverts back to its normal average, almost as if people return once again to the way things used to be. Incredible! Wasn't it a little less than a couple of weeks prior to Easter that people were drawn to Christ's suffering and death. Scripture readings throughout the season of Lent called us to contemplate how much Jesus sacrificed so that we can stand before God with a clear conscience. Holy Week meditations reflected on how much Jesus suffered and died for our sins. Also, how could we forget those glorious hymns on Easter morning! We sang them with much celebration and joy! *Christ the Lord is Risen Today! Easter People, Raise Your Voices! Up From Grave He Arose!* etc. We all celebrated Christ's spectacular resurrection and how he triumphed over the grave, as we declared that "death had been swallowed up in victory!" And now, we want to go back to "business as usual"? Sorry. For the person who is serious about following Jesus, there is no more business as usual in light of the Resurrection.

Initially for the ancient world, Jesus' resurrection did not make that much of a difference: Pontius Pilate was still governor over Judea. The Pharisees and Sadducees still argued over the same passages of Scripture. And the disciples—they went back to fishing. What? That's right. They went back to fishing. Yet, what about there's no more "business as usual" after the resurrection? That's true. Only for the disciples, what the Resurrection meant for them had not hit home yet. In Chapter 21 of John's gospel, Peter and the other disciples are out in their boat, fishing all night. After catching nothing, they are told by Jesus standing on the shoreline (whom they didn't recognize) to throw their nets over the right side of the boat and try again. When they did, the catch of fish was so large that they could not haul it in. Hmmm. Sounds fishy, no pun intended! After all, we've seen this before, haven't we? So had Peter. When he realizes that it is Jesus standing on the shore, he jumps into the water and swims the length of a football field to where Jesus has his Hibachi® ready to grill some more fish.

Ironically, this wasn't the first time Peter encountered Jesus in this way. The first time was also after a night of empty-handed fishing. Tired and weary, the disciples came in, only to have Jesus ask them to take him out a little farther and drop their nets on the right side of the boat. Like this last time, the catch was so great that they had difficulty hauling it in. This was when Peter dropped to his knees and begged Jesus to go away from him (Luke 5:1-11). Yet unlike the first meeting, Peter isn't pushing Jesus away. Instead, he's running, or rather swimming, toward him. What made the difference this time?

Perhaps it was that famous moment at Caesarea Philppi when Jesus asked Peter, *"Who do you say that I am?"* Peter replied confidently, *"You are the Christ!"* (Mark 8: 27-29). Perhaps the difference came following Jesus feeding the 5,000 (John 6:1-15), when many people turned away from Jesus. When asked if the original 12 disciples were going to desert Jesus too, Peter replied, *"Lord, to whom shall we go? You have the words of eternal life. We believe and know that you are the Holy One of God."* (John 6:60-69). Perhaps it was on the Mount of Transfiguration (Matthew 17:1-13) where Peter recalled the words, *"This is my Son, whom I love. With him I am well pleased. Listen to him."* Perhaps it was all of these encounters and more. Yet, I would like to suggest another possible explanation. Perhaps the reason why Peter couldn't wait to get to Jesus is because he knew he needed to be forgiven and restored by Jesus. That morning on the shores following the Resurrection, Jesus needed to restore Peter because after all, Peter did blow it. He denied he ever knew Jesus, just like Jesus said he would. Nevertheless, there's a subtle yet powerful shift in Jesus' words to Peter. In Luke 5:1-11, Jesus tells Peter to follow him so that he will catch men for the Kingdom of God. This time, Jesus asks Peter to take on the role of a shepherd of God's people. This was perhaps Peter's calling all along. . .to take care of and feed the people of God. In other words, the catch of fish has become for Peter a flock in need of nurture.

The story that follows this miraculous catch of fish is indeed a beautiful story of restoration, as Jesus asked Peter three times, *"Do you love me?"* Following Peter's denial, Jesus could have said, *"You see Peter, I told you so."* But he didn't. He simply asked if Peter loved him with a love that enabled him to remain in His love. The beauty of this passage comes in understanding the interplay of the New Testament Greek words used by both Jesus and Peter for *love*. For example, twice Jesus asked Peter if he loved (*agape*) him, and twice Peter replied that he did love (*phlieo*) him (John 21:15-18). Both times Jesus used the word *agape*, which implies the kind of love that seeks to fill or complete something in another person. The love people expressed in *agape* is not self-seeking, but rather other-seeking; to fill an emptiness or void in the life of another. *Phileo* love, on the other hand, is the kind of love found in friendships, and implies a desire to have the other person fill something that which is lacking in him/herself (Beck, 1999). By using *agape* love language, Jesus was asking Peter if his love was other-centered. It was not that Jesus lacked something that only Peter could fill, but rather, if Peter was able to love him with *agape* love, Peter then would also show *agape* love for others, namely the feeding and nurturing God's flock.

Metaphorically speaking, there's a big difference between catching fish and tending sheep. The work of both the evangelist and the pastor are vital to the work of God's kingdom on earth. Both require men and women who have *agape* love in their hearts for God and humanity. Both require helping people recognize Jesus' *agape* love for them. One stands at the beginning of that personal transformation as people realize a depth of God's love, mercy and grace that they never knew existed. The other, nurtures that on-going discovery of the ever-deepening work of transformation throughout people lives. Finally, both understand that without the Holy Spirit, transformation does not occur.

Whether or not Jesus loves us is a question we do not need to ask. Unfortunately, many times we do. He loves us, and will always love us, with an everlasting love (Jeremiah 31:3). However, when we look in the mirror the first thought we may be confronted with is: *"How could anyone love me? If others only knew the real me, I'm certain they would not want anything to do with me."* Remember. . . Jesus never saw Peter as hopeless. What he did see was potential, potential that would be realized through one simple touch of the Holy Spirit. Now, Peter needed to recognize this potential in himself in terms of what God can do in him and through him if only he was willing. If there were one thousand steps between us and Jesus, he would take nine-hundred ninety nine steps toward us. The one step he will never take is the one that belongs to us. That's all we ever need to take when seeking his forgiveness. If we will just turn around and take a step toward him in humility and repentance, the gap that once separated us will close.

I was in my middle-childhood years when the Jesus Movement of the early 1970's was in full swing. Once a week I would accompany my mother to the Wednesday night prayer services, which lasted for hours. I was enthralled by the joy and enthusiasm I heard from the singing and personal testimonies of God's grace. I remember one night quietly saying to myself, *"I wish I had what they had. I wish Jesus would become real to me."* Funny how even the quietest prayers can reach God's ears! Then, one Wednesday night I heard a song, whose words I had never forgotten. In fact, it was the first time in my life I felt Christ's forgiveness, grace and *agape* love wash over me:

For Those Tears I Died

You said you'd come and share all my sorrows
You said you'd be there for all my tomorrows
I came so close to sending you away
But just like you promised, you came here to stay
I just had to pray

Chorus
And Jesus said,
"Come to the water, stand by my side
I know you are thirsty, you won't be denied
I felt every tear drop, when in darkness you cried
And I strove to remind you,
It's for those tears I died"

Your goodness so great, I can't understand it
And dear Lord I know now that all this was planned
I know You're here now and always will be
Your love loosened my chains, and in You I'm free
But Jesus why me? Chorus

Jesus I give You, my heart and my soul
I know now without God, I'll never be whole
Savior, You opened all the right doors
And I thank You and praise You from earth's humble shores
Take me I'm Yours! Chorus
Words and Music by Marsha J. and Russ Stevens, © 1972
Communique Music, Inc.

Exercise 1:

(1) Begin by sitting comfortably. Take several deep breaths. When you are ready, read John 21:1-19 aloud. Silently meditate on these words. Make a note, which words resonate within your heart and soul. Perhaps you may want to do Exercise 2 and re-read *For Those Tears I Died*. Which sentences or phrase gets your attention? Sit with these for several minutes.

(2) As you re-read the passage, interact with the story. Reflect on the story and imagine yourself as Peter swimming toward Jesus. Imagine yourself as one of the disciples wondering what is going on between Peter and Jesus? What emotions are stirred in you as recall a time in your life when you faced the one betrayed with your words or actions?

(3) Re-read the passage. Ask God, "Where does this passage touch my life today?" With whom do you need ask forgiveness? Who do you need to forgive? What do you feel in your heart when you realize there have been times in your life when you have denied Jesus? Imagine you are standing on the beach with Jesus. What do you say to Jesus? What does Jesus say to you?

(4) Finally, ask yourself, "What it is that God wants me to do as a result of meditating on this passage?" What areas of my life do I need to probe the depth of God's love more for myself and in my relationships?

Exercise 2:

Sit quietly and read the words to the song, "*For Those Tears I Died.*" Perhaps you can play the song on a CD. Let the words sink into your heart as you embrace God's forgiveness and restoration:

Chapter 15

"What A Difference the Holy Spirit Makes!"
Acts 2:14-41

Then Peter stood up with the Eleven, raised his voice and addressed the crowd: "Fellow Jews and all who live in Jerusalem, let me explain this to you; listen carefully to what I say. These men are not drunk, as you suppose. It is only nine in the morning! No, this is what was spoken through the prophet Joel: 'In the last days, God says, I will pour out my Spirit on all people. Your sons and daughters will prophesy, your young men will see visions, your old men will dream dreams. Even on my servants, both men and women, I will pour out my Spirit in those days, and they will prophesy. I will show wonders in the heaven above and signs on the earth below, blood and fire and billows of smoke. The sun will be turned to darkness and the moon to blood before *the coming of the great and glorious day of the Lord. And everyone who calls on the name of the Lord will be saved.'*

"Men of Israel, listen to this: Jesus of Nazareth was a man accredited by God to you by miracles, wonders, and signs, which God did among you through him, as you yourselves know. This man was handed over to you by God's set purpose and foreknowledge; and you, with the help of wicked men, put him to death by nailing him to a cross. But God raised him from the dead, freeing him from the agony of death, because it was impossible for death to keep its hold on him. David said about him: 'I saw the Lord always before me. Because he is at my right hand, I will not be shaken. Therefore my heart is glad and my tongue rejoices; my body also will live in hope, because you will not abandon me to the grave, nor will you let your Holy One see decay. You have made known to me the paths of life; you will fill me with joy in your presence.'

"Brothers, I can tell you confidently that the patriarch David died and was buried, and that his tomb is here today. But he was a prophet and knew that God had promised him on oath that he would place one of his descendents on the throne. Seeing what was ahead, he spoke of the resurrection of Christ, that he was not abandoned to the grave, nor did his body see decay. God raised this Jesus to life, and we are all witnesses of the fact. Exalted to the right hand of God, he has received from the Father the promise of the Holy Spirit

and has poured out what you now see and hear. For David did not ascend to heaven and yet he said, 'The Lord said to my Lord: Sit at my right hand until I make your enemies a footstool for your feet.' Therefore let all Israel be assured of this: God has made this Jesus, whom you crucified, both Lord and Christ."

When the people heard this, they were cut to the heart and said to Peter and the other apostles, "Brothers, what shall we do?" Peter replied, "Repent and be baptized, everyone of you, in the name of Jesus Christ for the forgiveness of your sins. And you will receive the gift of the Holy Spirit. The promise is for you and your children and for all who are far off—for all whom the Lord our God will call." With many other words he warned them; and pleaded with them, "Save yourself from this corrupt generation." Those who accepted his message were baptized, and about three-thousand were added to their number that day.

Wow! Where did that come from? What happened to Peter? The last time we saw him, he was standing on the shore with Jesus, trying to grasp the impact of the resurrection for his life. Prior to that, Peter was trying to remain inconspicuous not only from the Roman guards who had carried Jesus away, but also from his fellow Jews who began to ask too many incriminating questions. However, now he's standing up and boldly proclaiming salvation through the resurrection of Jesus. Isn't amazing what happens when the Holy Spirit gets involved in our lives!

I'm sure we can all point to those before and after pictures from "infomercials" where people who were once overweight, have now experienced an incredible amount of weight loss or had successful results with hair-care products. Let's face it. It's hard to dispute pictures that show before and after results. In fact, these dramatic results speak for themselves to the transformation that is available to all. Peter also had a powerful transformation, not so much in the words he spoke, even though the people were convicted when they heard him. But perhaps the crowd was moved by how Peter spoke, i.e., with conviction. It doesn't take long after we starting reading this passage to see that this is certainly not the same Peter we encountered in the gospels! No. This time, something's different. This time, Peter's face was not red from eating crow, sticking his foot in his mouth, or even from feeling ashamed or guilty through his inappropriate, rash behavior. This time, Peter's face was red because he was filled with passion! He went from sticking his foot into his mouth and trying to figure things out, to proclaiming salvation through Jesus.

Understanding the Holy Spirit is often a difficult abstract for children, let alone adults, to grasp. After all, how do you relate the Spirit of God as "rushing wind" and "tongues of fire" to everyday life? When I talk about Pentecost I always use two relevant visual aides: Pinwheels and *Red Hots*® candies! Children love to watch the pinwheel spin with bright colors as they blow harder and harder (the candies make it fun for children to know what feels like to have their own special "tongues on fire"). As they watch their pinwheels turn, I invite them to remember how they may have watched trees sway as the wind blows. Truly, we do not know for sure where the wind comes from or where it goes (John 3:7), but we can see and feel its effect on our faces and other objects. The same is true with the Holy Spirit. We do not know exactly where the Holy Spirit comes or goes, but we can sense the Spirit's presence in our lives. In the Old Testament, the Holy Spirit is often referred to as the breath of God (*ruach*), but can also be interpreted as life, mind, wind and blast. For example, when "God's *Spirit* moved over the face of the earth. . ." (Genesis 1:2). The New Testament word for the Holy Spirit is *pneuma*, and also carries the same meaning of wind, breeze, life, and soul.

Pentecost was the Greek name given to the Jewish harvest festival of Shavuot, or the Feast of Weeks, that celebrated the grain harvest. Historically speaking, this festival was celebrated 50 days after the Exodus, on which God gave the Ten Commandments at Mount Sinai (Deuteronomy 16). This observance was also one of three feasts (the Feast of Unleavened Bread, the Feast of Weeks, and the Feast of Tabernacles) which required all Jewish men to come to

Jerusalem. No wonder people had come from all over the empire to celebrate. Even the disciples and believers in Christ, a group of about 120 people, had been in a room praying in Jerusalem. When the mighty breath of God rushed through the disciples, they were never the same again! Especially Peter. What a transformation!

Although it is next to impossible to sketch on paper what the Holy Spirit looks like, we can better identify with the Holy Spirit's effect in and through us. For some people, they describe the Holy Spirit as inspiration as when they discover truth in Scripture. Others describe the Holy Spirit as that ringing assurance when spiritual matters resonate within their own spirit. Still, others may describe the Holy Spirit as the One who imparts spiritual gifts and graces people need to carry on the work of Christ in the world. Whatever descriptors people use to talk about the Holy Spirit, one thing is for certain: People can tell the difference. For example, before Pentecost, the disciples were scared to death to tell others about Jesus. Doing so was a good way to get into serious trouble, because the people who had killed Jesus in the first place also wanted to get rid of everybody who was claiming Jesus had risen from the dead. As a result, when they met together, they did so secretly and behind closed and locked doors. Yet, after they received the Holy Spirit in such a powerful way, they were emboldened to live the gospel message in life-changing ways. From that moment on, people did not just hear the good news of Jesus Christ; they were drawn to him by witnessing the radical transformation this message had in the lives of the disciples.

For us today, we receive the Holy Spirit through faith to also enable us to be the presence of Christ in the world. We are indeed his hands that reach out to the disenfranchised. We are the ones who offer hope and spirituality to those down in the cracks whom society describes as unloveable, untouchable and unreachable. We are all different; yet, all of our gifts and graces to serve come from one Holy Spirit. If there's one aspect of looking at Peter's life that communicates meaning, it is to understand that the purpose of the Holy Spirit is not to make us the same, but to make us whole. Jesus indeed encountered many different types of personalities. Just look at the disciples! Perhaps you have struggled with this yourself? Perhaps you wished God would make you into a person just like your favorite evangelist or pastor or best friend. Sorry to burst your bubble, but God does not do such things. Instead, God's desire is for us to be made into the image of Christ. Does this mean that God wants us to "scrap" our personalities in order to be the hands and feet of Christ? No. On the contrary, God uses all types of people in this world just like God used Peter, Andrew, Paul, John Wesley, Francis, Mother Teresa, Thomas Merton, you and me. For those training to become professional counselors, I tell my students that they should find a population they have a desire to work with. Initially, some students experience frustration because they believe they can counsel anyone, regardless of the circumstances. While this is true, especially if they embrace the value of their pastoral presence, most discover they are better equipped with certain gifts and graces to work with one population over another. For example, some students find great satisfaction counseling the prison population or within a battered women's shelter, but find difficulty counseling people in hospice or bereavement. On the other hand, there are counselors I know who are content to work with teenagers in a high-school setting, but become completely unnerved if they counsel people in substance recovery agencies. Why are some people better suited to counsel specific clients against others? Perhaps they have had similar backgrounds themselves? Perhaps they feel led to work with the "brokenhearted" in society? Perhaps they have the type of personality needed by God through whom He can extend healing grace? All of the above. Grow where God has planted you. It truly doesn't matter who plants or who waters, as long as God brings the increase! Just ask Peter.

Exercise:

(1) Begin by sitting comfortably. Take several deep breaths. When you are ready, read Acts 2:14-41 aloud. Silently meditate on these words. Make a note, which words resonate within your heart and soul. What sentence or phrase gets your attention? Sit with these for several minutes. Perhaps you would like to meditate on the words to the hymn, "Here I Am, Lord" and discover where you identify with these words.

(2) As you re-read the passage, interact with the story. Reflect on the story and imagine yourself being there with the other disciples, hearing the sound of rushing wind all around you. Imagine, the wind on your face and blowing through your hair. Take several a deep breaths and allow this rushing wind to fill your lungs. Exhale slowly each time.

(3) Re-read the passage. Ask God, "Where does this passage touch my life today?" Where does Peter's speech touch you in your heart and soul? Where have you been transformed in your perceptions, reasoning, and faith? What areas of your life still needs to come under God's control.

(4) Finally, ask yourself, "What it is that God wants me to do as a result of meditating on this passage?" What areas of my life do I need to probe the depth of God's love more for myself and in my relationships?

<u>Here I Am, Lord</u>
Words and Music by Daniel L Schutte (1981)

I, the Lord of sea and sky,
I have heard my people cry.
All who dwell in dark and sin,
My hand will save.

<u>Chorus</u>
Here I am, Lord. Is it I, Lord?
I have heard you calling in the night.
I will go, Lord, if you lead me.
I will hold your people in my heart.

I, who made the stars of night,
I will make their darkness bright.
Who will bear my light to them?
Whom shall I send?

<u>Chorus</u>

Here I am, Lord. Is it I, Lord?

I have heard you calling in the night.

I will go, Lord, if you lead me.

I will hold your people in my heart.

I, the Lord of snow and rain,

I have borne my people's pain.

I have wept for love of them.

They turn away.

<u>Chorus</u>

Here I am, Lord. Is it I, Lord?

I have heard you calling in the night.

I will go, Lord, if you lead me.

I will hold your people in my heart.

I will break their hearts of stone,

Give them hearts for love alone.

I will speak my words to them.

Whom shall I send?

continued

Chorus

Here I am, Lord. Is it I, Lord?

I have heard you calling in the night.

I will go, Lord, if you lead me.

I will hold your people in my heart.

I, the Lord of wind and flame,

I will send the poor and lame.

I will set a feast for them.

My hand will save.

Chorus

Here I am, Lord. Is it I, Lord?

I have heard you calling in the night.

I will go, Lord, if you lead me.

I will hold your people in my heart.

Finest bread I will provide,

'Til their hearts be satisfied.

I will give my life to them.

Whom shall I send?

<u>Chorus</u>

Here I am, Lord. Is it I, Lord?

I have heard you calling in the night.

I will go, Lord, if you lead me.

I will hold your people in my heart.

REFERENCES

Beck, J.R. (1999). *Jesus & personality theory: Exploring the five-factor model.* Downers Grove, IL: Intervarsity Press.

Black, K. (1996). *A healing homiletic: Preaching and disability.* Nashville: Abingdon Press.

Crane, S. (2004). *The red badge of courage.* Smyrna, DE: Prestwick House, Inc.

Cunxin, L. (2003). *Mao's last dancer.* New York: G.P. Putnam's Sons.

De Mello, A. (1984). *The song of the bird.* New York: Doubleday.

Doblmeier, M. (2007). *The power of forgiveness* (DVD). New York: First Run Features.

Goffman, E. (1986). *Stigma: Notes on the management of spoiled identity.* New York: Simon and Schuster, Inc.

Hazard, D. (1994). *You set my spirit free: A 40-day journey in the company of St. John of the cross.* Minneapolis: Bethany House Publishers.

Hiedinger, J.V. (1986). *Basic methodist beliefs: An evangelical view.* Anderson, IN: Bristol House, Ltd.

Knox, R and Oakley, M (trans.) (1959). *Thomas a' Kempis: The imitation of Christ.* NY: Sheed and Ward.

Myss, C. (2002). *Spiritual Madness: The necessity of meeting God in darkness* (Audio CD). Louisville, CO: Sounds True, Inc.

Merton, T. (1971). *Contemplative prayer.* New York: Image Books.

Moltmann, J. Bowden, J (Translator), Wilson, R.A. (Translator) (1993). *The crucified God:*

The cross of Christ as the foundation and criticism of Christian theology. Minneapolis, MN:Augsburg Fortress Publishers.

Nouwen, H. (2006). *Can you drink from the cup?* Notre Dame, IN: Ave Maria Press.

Starr, M. (2002). *Dark night of the soul: St. John of the cross: A new translation and introduction.* New York: Penguin Books.

Tangney, J. P. and Dearing, R. L. (2002). *Shame and guilt.* New York: Guildford Press.

Thompson, Francis (1978). *Hound of heaven and other poems.* Belair, CA: Branden Books.

Tutu, D. (2000). *No future without forgiveness.* New York: Image Books.

Wenham, G.J. (1994). *Leviticus: New international commentary on the Old Testament.* Minneapolis: Wm. B. Eerdmans Publishing Company.

Wicks, R.J. (2007). *Touching the holy: Ordinariness, self-esteem and friendship.* Notre Dame, IN: Sorin Books.

Printed in the United States
218790BV00001B/18/P